POPE FRANCIS AND CAMPUS MINISTRY

POPE FRANCIS AND CAMPUS MINISTRY

A DIALOGUE

James J. Bacik

FOREWORD BY
Richard R. Gaillardetz

Paulist Press
New York / Mahwah, NJ

Library of Congress Cataloging-in-Publication Data
Names: Bacik, James J., 1936- author.
Title: Pope Francis and campus ministry : a dialogue / James J. Bacik.
Description: New York : Paulist Press, 2018. | Includes bibliographical references.
Identifiers: LCCN 2017030136 (print) | LCCN 2018002759 (ebook) | ISBN 9781587687068 (ebook) | ISBN 9780809153398 (pbk. : alk. paper)
Subjects: LCSH: Church work with college students—Catholic Church. | Church work with college students—United States. | Francis, Pope, 1936—Influence.
Classification: LCC BX2347.8.S8 (ebook) | LCC BX2347.8.S8 B33 2018 (print) | DDC 259/.24088282—dc23
LC record available at https://lccn.loc.gov/2017030136

ISBN 978-0-8091-5339-8 (paperback)
ISBN 978-1-58768-706-8 (e-book)

Published by Paulist Press
997 Macarthur Boulevard
Mahwah, New Jersey 07430

www.paulistpress.com

Printed and bound in the
United States of America

For Pam Meseroll
My good friend and longtime colleague in campus ministry, who
combines a tender compassionate heart and astute practical wisdom
in a life of generous service empowered by the Gracious Mystery

CONTENTS

CONTENTS

FOREWORD

This book on campus ministry is informed by the wisdom and pastoral experience of two quite different but equally extraordinary pastors. They were born within two months of each other, and between them they have over one hundred years of experience as priests of the church. The Second Vatican Council had a decisive impact on both. One of them is Rev. James J. Bacik, a diocesan priest, respected theologian, an expert in the theology of Karl Rahner, and a veritable legend in Catholic campus ministry. The other is a Jesuit from South America with whom readers are more likely to be familiar, Jorge Bergoglio, the current bishop of Rome, who in 2013 took the name Francis.

Fr. Bacik, the author of this book, has spent decades in the field of campus ministry. He was the ghostwriter for the United States Conference of Catholic Bishops' pastoral letter on campus ministry and has won numerous national awards for his groundbreaking work. This book marks, in many ways, a retrospective on his own ministerial career and on the development of Catholic campus ministry over the last four decades. His unique ministerial and theological background has prepared him well to offer such a compelling, challenging, and comprehensive vision of the possibilities and challenges facing Catholic campus ministry.

One of the principal tasks of campus ministry concerns the pastoral care of the various segments of the university community: the administrators, the faculty, and, of course, the students. Bacik offers an extended exploration of what this pastoral care entails. He explores the challenges of creating an authentic faith community in a university context and considers the responsibility campus ministers have for helping the members of that university community to grow in their faith and to form their consciences in ways that enable them to meet the challenges of our time.

One of this volume's most important contributions, however, lies in Bacik's conviction that campus ministry must do more than offer a spiritual oasis for Catholic college students. Catholic campus ministry must speak to the very culture of higher education. The greatest gift that any university, public or private, can offer our society is what Martha Nussbaum calls the "cultivation of humanity."[1] This goal is embraced wholeheartedly by our own Catholic tradition. As our American bishops observed, "By teaching people to think critically and to search for the truth, colleges and universities help to humanize our world."[2] Catholic Christianity has always held dear a form of Christian humanism that can be of service to all of humankind. Catholicism dares to hold that Christ "reveals humanity to itself and brings to light its very high calling."[3] One way of describing this cultivation of humanity, as Bacik reminds us, is the pursuit of wisdom. The distinction between wisdom and knowledge is an ancient one in our Catholic heritage, going back, at least, to St. Augustine. In our technological world, it is a distinction that has become more important than ever. By wisdom, here, I mean the kind of reflection that looks for the whole, the connectedness of things. This is, after all, the root meaning of the term *catholic* (from the Greek, *kat holou*), "pertaining to the whole."

The Catholic commitment to the cultivation of humanity and the pursuit of wisdom offers a helpful foundation for a vision of higher education that must inform the university today, public and private. Wisdom is concerned with questions of truth, to be sure, but even more so it is concerned with questions of meaning: How does my understanding of our world give meaning to my existence? As such, the quest for wisdom can undergird such disparate academic concerns as an astrophysicist developing new technologies for determining the existence of planets in distant star systems, and business professors analyzing the role of demographic studies in marketing research. There are significant forces in higher education that would justify the isolated pursuit of these academic inquiries in strictly utilitarian terms, for example, their success in garnering federal funding for the university or in placing students in a competitive job market. Yet a university that sees itself as a wisdom community committed to facilitating the human search for meaning will frame these pursuits in considerably different ways. The gift the Catholic tradition can offer universities

Foreword

in our country, private and public, is the reminder that the quest for knowledge must be placed in service of the quest for wisdom.

Throughout this volume, Bacik brings his capacious vision of campus ministry into productive dialogue with the remarkable, pastoral vision of Pope Francis. His insightful interpretation of this pontificate is worth the price of the book alone! Bacik sees in our first Jesuit pope a pastoral style uniquely suited to campus ministry. Pope Francis has consistently called for a "culture of encounter," a culture that is committed to patiently listening to the concerns and insights of others. This culture of encounter demands that Christians leave their places of security and move to the "peripheries," meeting people where they live. In taking his papal name from St. Francis of Assisi, he has invoked the deep spirit of humility associated with that great medieval saint. It is a humility that leads him to admit his own personal failings and the failings of his church. His Christocentrism is not dogmatic but pastoral, oriented toward the concrete shape that following the way of Jesus of Nazareth takes for those who would call themselves his disciples. These characteristics, Bacik argues, shine new light on the work of campus ministry.

In this volume, the reader benefits from a rich and rewarding conversation between two wise pastors offering tremendous insight and hope for the future of campus ministry.

Dr. Richard R. Gaillardetz
The Joseph Professor of Catholic Systematic
Theology at Boston College

INTRODUCTION

How will Pope Francis affect campus ministry in the United States in the decades ahead? This book explores this important question by setting up a dialogue between campus ministry, as I have known it for the last three decades, and Pope Francis, who has already made a remarkable impact on the world and the church by word and example. It presents many of the pope's major teachings, highlighting their practical relevance for ministry in today's church.

For more than fifty years, I have been blessed with the opportunity to be involved in the exciting world of campus ministry. In the early 1960s, my bishop sent me to one of the first summer training sessions for campus ministers, held at the University of Colorado, where I met the impressive leaders of the Newman movement and gained an initial impression of the creative ministry occurring on campuses around the country. During that decade, I taught classes at a local nursing school in Sandusky, Ohio, where I got to know something of the spiritual journey of dedicated young women. In 1971, my bishop appointed me associate pastor of St. Thomas More University Parish serving Bowling Green State University, where I worked as a campus minister for twelve years, followed by thirty years as a pastor for Corpus Christi University Parish serving the University of Toledo.

During the 1980s, I worked several years for the American bishops as the writer for the editorial committee charged with producing a pastoral letter on campus ministry. An initial draft effort entitled "The Quest for Wisdom: The Church in Dialogue with Higher Education" was the forerunner to *Empowered by the Spirit: Campus Ministry Faces the Future*, which was published in 1985.

Over the years, I have written many articles on various aspects of campus ministry based on my own experience. Some of them are

1

collected in this book, especially those connected with the construction and application of *Empowered by the Spirit*, which has guided campus ministry in the United States since its publication. I have purposely not edited the articles so that they function as a history of the development of campus ministry. That strategy leaves many repetitions, but it also indicates my own reading of the successes and challenges faced by the church on campus since the mid-1980s. Each article is preceded by a section called "Context," designed to help the reader understand the historical setting of the material, and each is followed by a section entitled "Dialogue with Francis," which explores how the pope's style and teaching might affect the direction of campus ministry in the years ahead. This approach aligns with that of Francis, who insists that dialogue is not just a practical strategy but flows from the thrust of the gospel. For him, dialogue with "historical memory" is a way to prepare for a better future. Since the pope has not yet made a major statement on campus ministry, the material is drawn from various sources: his own example of authentic simplicity and bold pastoral initiatives; his talks to young adults, seminarians, educators, and ordained clergy; his apostolic exhortation *The Joy of the Gospel*; his encyclical, *Laudato Si'*; and his major addresses during his historic visit to the United States. Each of these sections envisions specific ways the church on campus can put the vision and style of Francis into practice.

In some ways, the Francis effect is already evident on some campuses: for example, an increasing number of Christian service programs designed to give students direct contact with persons living in poverty; and more efforts to practice the ecological virtues that promote care for the environment. The long-term effect of Francis on the church remains part of an essentially unknown future, subject to many historical variables. It is clear, however, that he has already made a significant impact and that campus ministry, with its typical openness and creativity, can be an important bearer of his legacy.

Hopefully, this book will be helpful to those directly concerned with the church on campus: leaders who find affirmation for their current ministry and suggestions for new initiatives; bishops and diocesan directors who gain historical perspective on campus ministry and a deeper appreciation of its importance to the church as a whole; potential donors who expect results from their contributions; parents who want their collegiate sons and daughters to maintain their Catholic heritage and to grow in the faith; faculty members who want programming that helps them appropriate their faith and develop spiritually; and dedicated student leaders who are looking for ways to get more students involved.

The book will also be of interest to Catholics who want to know more about Pope Francis and his hopes for the church. Reflecting on him from the perspective of campus ministry can reveal aspects of his personality and teaching missed by more secular approaches and by more systematic treatments of his theology and pastoral practice.

The six parts are built around my articles written over the past three decades. The first part recounts the process of writing "The Quest for Wisdom" and includes the actual text of the first part of this earlier draft document, which is published here for the first time with the permission of the United States Conference of Catholic Bishops. By his consistent emphasis on the church as a missionary community, Pope Francis reminds campus ministry of its important mission to help humanize the academic world.

Part two deals with the pastoral letter, *Empowered by the Spirit*, suggesting some theological perspectives that can enrich the practice of its six ministerial functions: forming community, appropriating the faith, forming the Christian conscience, educating for justice, facilitating personal development, and developing leaders for the future. These functions have structured the practice of campus ministry for over three decades. Each one can be enhanced by the example and teaching of Francis. Facilitating personal development, for instance, can find inspiration in the pope's authentic simplicity that has made such an impact on people all over the world. Under the influence of Francis, campus ministers will continue to expand their Christian service programs that involve personal encounters with persons on the margins and subsequent reflection on the experience.

Part three suggests that campus ministry can function more effectively by developing a better understanding of the millennial generation it serves. Francis encourages us to reach out to young adults with the merciful forgiveness of the Father, the concrete example of Christ, and the joyful hope of the Holy Spirit. The pope, who uses Twitter regularly, also provides us with a telling critique of the technocratic culture and, specifically, of the ambivalent impact of social media.

The articles in part four contain practical suggestions for forming community, considered by many campus ministers as crucial to the success of their other programming. Francis provides an important perspective on community building by turning our attention to the family as the primary community, the building block of society, the place where we learn fundamental values and Christian virtues. His insightful analysis of married love in his apostolic exhortation *Amoris Laetitia* is especially helpful in preparing students for marriage. The pope's family perspective also provides some concrete imagery: for example, the church on campus tries to provide a family atmosphere, a home away from home, where all are welcomed and each person is treasured in their uniqueness.

The fifth part contains one article on the attitudes, skills, and knowledge that educated Catholic college graduates should have, and another on practical suggestions for establishing Chairs of Catholic Studies at public universities. Although Francis is not a professional theologian, he has given us some helpful theological perspectives and concrete images: for instance, an anthropology that emphasizes our relationship not only to God and our fellow humans but also to nature; and an ecclesiology that sees the church as a field hospital caring for the seriously wounded. The pope also reminds us that facts are more important than ideas, and that living the Christian life is more important than reflecting on it. This chapter contains a summary of his brilliant treatment of liturgical preaching and an application of his understanding of church as a communion that courageously goes forth into the world.

Part six includes a section on social justice taken from "The Quest for Wisdom" and an account of students serving those in need. It is in this area of social justice that we can expect a profound impact by Francis as the church on campus explores and implements his groundbreaking encyclical *Laudato Si'*, summarized in this chapter in both its environmental and its social ecology.

The epilogue warns against drawing Francis into a kind of "papalism" that expects too much of the pope and too little of the people of God. The dialogue with Francis works best if it generates creative pastoral approaches attuned to local situations.

Those of who find inspiration and hope in Pope Francis are looking for ways to maintain and expand his influence. As this book demonstrates, campus ministry is a great vehicle for appropriating and creatively applying the example and teaching of this formidable man and remarkable pope who has captured the imagination of so many around the world.

I

THE
QUEST
FOR
WISDOM

1

BACKGROUND AND CONTEXT

In 1983, the year the American bishops published their influential pastoral letter, *The Challenge of Peace*, they also decided to address the issue of campus ministry. Bishop William Friend, assisted by Fr. Joseph Kenna representing the United States Conference of Catholic Bishops (USCCB), was put in charge of organizing an editorial committee charged with formulating a document for approval by the bishops. The committee contacted me (through the persuasive intermediary, Fr. Donald Cozzens, who has played such a crucial role in the reform of the priesthood) about collaborating with them on writing the proposed pastoral. At the time, I was a co-pastor, along with my friend and colleague, Fr. Dan Zak, of Corpus Christi University Parish serving the University of Toledo. After meeting with the committee in Washington, I agreed to take on the extra assignment that occupied my attention from that day, June 3, 1983, until the final draft, *Empowered by the Spirit*, was published on November 15, 1985. The committee, convinced that we needed broad consultation with campus ministers, students, and leaders of higher education, organized listening sessions around the country. We also gathered helpful ideas from written responses to questionnaires, especially ones from presidents of universities who indicated that they welcomed a word from the church on higher education. These consultations were extremely valuable in my task of writing various drafts of the proposed pastoral incorporating the best thoughts of the committee.

The following article, written in April 1986 but never published in this form, summarizes the process of developing an early draft of the pastoral and identifies some of the content.[1] The issues treated remain a concern today and the wisdom of the church is still called to respond to them.

DEVELOPING A PASTORAL LETTER

In 1983, a committee of four bishops and eight campus ministers, chaired by Bishop William Friend, began, at the direction of the Catholic bishops, to work on a proposed pastoral letter on campus ministry. During the early meetings, it became clear that the proposed letter could not address the problems of campus ministry without looking at the entire academic environment in which this ministry is carried out. Campus ministers serve students, faculty members, and administrators whose lives are caught up in the concerns of the academic world. Fidelity to the gospel demands that those who minister on campuses understand the world of higher education and work with others to improve and renew it.

Consequently, the committee became convinced that the proposed pastoral would have to address the situation of higher education. The church would have to hear the voices of those vitally concerned about our colleges and universities and respond from the perspective of Christian faith and a traditional concern for the dignity and worth of every human being.

When the committee decided to address the concerns of higher education, it was aware of major studies, such as "Three Thousand Futures," the final report of the Carnegie Council on Policy Studies in Higher Education issued in 1982. However, there was a general feeling that we needed more direct information from people concerned with the future of our colleges and universities. To this end, we solicited suggestions from many students, faculty members, and campus ministers. Especially important to our work were the nearly three hundred responses we received from presidents and elected faculty leaders representing institutions of higher education from all fifty states that informed us of their hopes and concerns.

Based on this material, the committee hoped that the initial draft document would be a fresh voice that would help renew the debate on higher education in our country. What we did not know was that at least three other groups were also preparing statements on higher education. Thus, after the bulk of the first draft of the proposed pastoral was completed, three other very significant documents on higher education appeared. Our envisioned fresh voice was now happily joined with others addressing similar issues.

In October 1984, the study group on "Conditions of Excellence in American Education" issued a series of twenty-seven specific recommendations for improving the quality of higher education in a report appropriately entitled, "Involvement in Learning: Realizing the Potential of American Higher Education."[2] The study group, which included well-known authors in the field such as Alexander Astin and Howard Bowen, cited many warning signals that indicate that higher education is not living up to its ideal and potential. For example, student performances on eleven of fifteen major Subject Area Tests of the Graduate Record Examinations declined between 1964 and 1982. The warning signals alert us to the fact that student learning, curriculum coherence, faculty morale, and academic standards do not measure up to our expectations.

Their prescriptions for improving this situation center on increasing student involvement in the learning process. Research suggests that the more intensely students engage in their own education, the greater their personal growth, their satisfaction with their college experience, and their persistence in becoming lifelong learners. Involved students put considerable energy into studying, participate in student organizations, and interact frequently with faculty members and other students. There are many ways to encourage this involvement. Administrators should ensure that first-year students are exposed to the best teachers, are given the opportunity for personal contact with instructors, and have access to well-trained advisers. Professors should utilize active teaching techniques such as small-group discussions, intern programs, collaborative research projects, class presentations and debate, and supervised independent study.

Students are advised to: seek out a particular faculty member who will serve as a mentor, advisor, and friend; get involved in some campus organization that will enable them to make use of material learned in courses; contribute to the life of the campus through student government, peer counseling, and so on; attend full-time classes for at least part of their student career; seek work on campus if it is necessary to have a job; do at least one internship and independent study during their collegiate days; use electives to explore fields in which their knowledge is limited; and insist on participating in regular evaluation of their institution's programs and environment.

To move toward academic excellence, colleges and universities must have clear, publicly stated expectations of the knowledge, capacity, and skills that students should develop during their collegiate careers. The report suggests that all bachelor's degree recipients have at least two full years of liberal education, that they develop capacities of analysis, problem solving, communication, and synthesis, and the ability to integrate knowledge from various disciplines. Each institution should develop their curriculum around the knowledge, capacities, and skills that students are expected to develop and find instruments designed and implemented by faculty and deans for assessing whether these goals are attained.

A crucial element in accomplishing educational reform includes finding institutional means of encouraging professors to put more effort into educating undergraduate students. They must be rewarded in terms of compensation, promotion, and tenure for good teaching and not just for research and publication, as is so often the case today. They must be better prepared in graduate school for teaching undergraduates, be given professional help to improve, especially at the beginning of their teaching careers, and be evaluated regularly by students and peers.

Many other valuable recommendations are included in this report. They are all designed to refocus the administrative decisions and faculty effort toward the actively involved learning of undergraduate students.

In November 1984, William Bennett, using findings from a study group concerned with the state of the humanities in higher education, published a forty-two-page report entitled "To Reclaim a Legacy."[3] His indictment of higher education is harsh. College graduates lack "even the most rudimentary knowledge about the history, literature, art and philosophic foundations of their nation and civilization." His focus is on the humanities, which should be "at the heart of the college curriculum," but have been diluted or almost completely lost. For example, a student can obtain a bachelor's degree from 72 percent of all American colleges and universities without having studied American literature or history. Bennett places the blame not on students, nor on the vocationalism popular in the culture. Rather, he indicts the administrators and faculty who have lost their nerve in the face of cultural trends and student pressures, and have therefore failed "to protect and transmit a legacy our students deserve to know." His prescriptions for reversing the decline in undergraduate education center on curriculum reforms that reflect a clear, articulated vision of what constitutes an educated person. For him, this means more in-depth study of history, philosophy, languages, and literature and a commitment on the part of faculties to put aside narrow interests and collaborate on a core of common studies. Study of the humanities is essential because they raise the great enduring questions and enable individuals to participate in a common culture. The humanities, which include language, literature, linguistics, history, jurisprudence, philosophy, archeology, comparative religion, ethics, the fine arts, and the humanistic social sciences, should be taught by professors who have mastered the material and can bring it to life for the students. A good curriculum will enable students to study the humanities throughout their collegiate career and will balance wide reading with careful in-depth study of a few important original texts. Bennett notes that he does not want to dictate anyone's curriculum, but he does list over thirty authors whom he thinks have shaped the Western mind, including Plato, Dickens, Marx, Twain, and Faulkner. The curriculum should reflect the vision of an educated person who has a knowledge of the origins and development of Western civilization, an understanding of the most significant ideas and debates in the history of philosophy, proficiency in a foreign language, and some familiarity with at least one non-Western culture. The key is to have a course of studies in which all students share a carefully designed sequence of humanities courses arranged in logical progression. Each course should build on the previous ones and involve the reading of important original texts. Bennett calls upon presidents of colleges and universities to be more concerned about academic affairs, to articulate institutional goals and standards, and to understand that good teaching is rewarded in hiring, promotion, and tenure decisions. The Bennett report wants to reclaim the legacy of liberal education by exposing undergraduate students to a systematic study of the humanities, especially through the primary texts that have shaped Western culture. Consequently, he thinks that colleges and universities will accept again their "vital role as conveyor of the accumulated wisdom of our civilization."[4]

A third major study entitled "Integrity in the College Curriculum: A Report to the Academic Community" appeared in February

1985 under the names of a nineteen-member committee of the Association of American Colleges.[5] They decry the decline and devaluation of the undergraduate degree that is manifested in a curriculum that has become a supermarket where "students are shoppers and professors are merchants of learning." The major taken by undergraduates is "little more than a gathering of courses taken in one department, lacking structure and depth." The general education requirements lack rational coherence while electives are used "to fatten majors and diminish breadth."

The report places great responsibility for this situation on "the transformation of the professors from teachers concerned with the characters and minds of their students" to professionals who are more interested in research and more committed to their discipline than to the life of the institution and the well-being of students. They have abdicated their responsibility to maintain a coherent curriculum. Over time, the traditional course of studies has been abandoned, and student interest has determined course offerings.

Just as faculties are at the center of the problem, so they are crucial to a solution. This report joins the other two in insisting that faculty members must be trained to teach and rewarded for good teaching. The enemy of good teaching is not research, but rather the notion that it is the only worthy or legitimate task for faculty members. Thus, the authors of "Integrity in the College Curriculum" regard research and teaching as mutually enriching. "The finest teachers are often the best researchers." The report suggests that the traditional curriculum committee should determine how the wisdom of faculty members is brought to bear on the overall course of studies. This committee would keep institutional goals from being subverted by narrow departmental interests. It would celebrate superb teaching and call attention to good teaching practices that could be adopted by others.

The report's concrete suggestions for achieving a coherent curriculum are not based on reading certain texts, as Bennett suggested, but on providing intellectual, aesthetic, and philosophic learning experiences that will enable graduates to achieve the kind of skills necessary to live responsibly and joyfully as individuals and democratic citizens. They list nine experiences, skills, and ways of understanding. Most importantly, students in all courses must be enabled to reason well, think critically, judge wisely, and imagine creatively. Additionally, they must become literate by mastering the skills of writing, reading, speaking, and listening;

learn to understand numerical data and make good judgments about arguments that depend on numbers and statistics; gain historical consciousness that enables them to appreciate complexity and ambiguity as part of the human condition; master the methodology, value, and limits of the scientific method; investigate value questions and gain the capacity to make informed and responsible moral choices; develop an appreciation of the fine and performing arts; be exposed to international and multicultural experiences; and, finally, have the opportunity to study a particular subject in depth.

The report develops this last point at greater length. In-depth study does not occur simply because many courses are taken in one area. Rather, it is based on understanding a discipline's methodology, its range of topics, characteristic questions, and arguments, and its history and philosophical presuppositions. In-depth study involves taking courses in sequence and working with primary texts, documents, artifacts, and works of art. Such a study can be carried on not only in the liberal arts, but in all academic disciplines, including the sciences, interdisciplinary studies, and professional and vocational fields.

The report insists that colleges and universities be accountable to students, state legislatures, and the public at large by explicitly stating their goals for students and then devising ways of evaluating progress toward those goals. Finally, it echoes suggestions for improving the performance of professors in the classroom, which we already noted from the other documents.

The essence of this third report is found in its appeal to administrators and faculty to "lead us away from the declining and devalued bachelor's degree that now prevails to a new era of curriculum coherence," in which students will develop the kind of skills necessary for responsible citizenship and an enjoyable life.

On March 21, 1985, the bishops released the first draft of their pastoral entitled "The Quest for Wisdom: The Church in Dialogue with Higher Education." Based on our survey, we noted that the draft document appeared amid a national debate on the quality of undergraduate education. Certain questions arise: How does the bishops' document compare with the other reports? Does it have anything distinctive to offer? How can the first draft be improved in the light of the current debate? Note that the following responses to these questions come from the perspective of one who was closely involved in the preparation of this first draft of the bishops' document.

The draft document concentrates on the concerns in higher education that have the clearest relationship to the work of the church on campus. Through extensive consultation with people in the academic world, five major areas of concern emerged.

THE NATURE AND PURPOSE OF HIGHER EDUCATION

As the other three reports indicated, we suffer from the lack of a clear, articulated vision of what higher education is trying to accomplish. In response, the pastoral begins by sketching out a vision of the dignity of human beings and the dynamic character of human existence that is derived primarily from the Second Vatican Council's document on *The Church in the Modern World*. The pastoral pulls together the various strains of this philosophical anthropology under the ideal notion of "the life of wisdom." Based on this ideal, "Human beings achieve a richer personal synthesis which is the fulfillment of the pursuit of truth; discover the highest principles which integrate all knowledge; and learn to combine the theoretical with the practical, self-fulfillment with a concern for the common good, and knowledge with the light of love."[6] The quest for wisdom becomes the theme of the entire document and the perspective from which all the concerns are addressed. Thus, higher education has the overarching task of preparing students for the life of wisdom. Pope John Paul II further specified the task: "to lead the mind to truth, so that it will not succumb to the deadly infection of relativism; to lead the will to the good by rescuing it from an empty and deadened anarchism; to convert the entire person to the objectivity of values, in opposition to every form of subjectivism."[7]

Thus, the pastoral letter speaks from a clear perspective based on the dignity and social character of human existence. It does not hesitate to present a notion that is the life of wisdom, to guide the discussion on the nature of higher education, and to organize the efforts to renew it. The initial feedback on the letter indicated that this is one of the strengths of the document and part of its unique contribution.

QUALITY

The very existence of the various reports testifies to the common feeling that higher education is not living up to its potential. The pastoral letter concurs in this judgment, although it notes the positive contributions of higher education as well. The bishops' primary suggestion for improving the situation is to place the well-being of students in the center of the educational enterprise. "Students are not just commodities but persons with potential to be discovered and developed."[8] In policy decisions, curriculum design, and the conduct of professors, we must be mindful of the welfare of students. Students are also reminded of their responsibilities to get more involved in the classroom and the campus. It is in this section that the draft supports the Carnegie Council's call for greater state aid to private education and for a system of tuition scholarships that can be used at any college or university.

This section of the letter would benefit the most from the concrete suggestions found in the other three reports. More could be said about involvement of students, the training and evaluation of professors, the need for policy changes by trustees and administrators, the kind of skills, capacities, and knowledge that we expect students to have, the construction of a coherent curriculum, and the importance of solid evaluation procedures.

BALANCE

Under this heading, the pastoral discusses the "overemphasis on practical competency or vocational training to the great detriment of the cognitive goals of developing critical thinking and a cultivated mind." It also decries the almost exclusive concern for the empirical methods sometimes employed even by the liberal arts. More specifically, the letter notes that religion courses are not found in adequate numbers in the curriculum of most colleges and universities. "As a result society suffers because most college graduates have a meager knowledge of the world's great religious traditions and especially the Judeo-Christian tradition, which has helped shape our western culture."[9]

In response to these imbalances, the pastoral letter draws on the thought of Cardinal Newman to make the case for a liberal education that disciplines the intellect, provides the ability to relate and synthesize ideas, and helps to develop the whole person. The document claims that a complete liberal education includes the objective study of the history, teachings, and practices of the various world religions, especially the Judeo-Christian tradition. It goes on to argue: "Colleges and universities have a duty to teach about religion because religious knowledge has an inherent value, constitutes a legitimate academic discipline, is a part of our cultural heritage, can broaden understanding and tolerance of others' values, and can serve as an integrating principle for the rest of learning. Students have a right to know about religion because it is absolutely essential for understanding themselves and the world."[10]

In this section, the letter echoes the general call in the other reports for greater emphasis on the humanities and for approaches that cultivate critical thinking. It sounds a distinctive note by insisting on the value of religious literacy in a well-rounded education. "The life of wisdom needs the focus and breath which comes from religious knowledge."[11] Here the bishops speak for a traditional wisdom that has been largely lost in the secular world.

VALUES AND ETHICS

The pastoral letter notes many ethical and value questions that arise in the academic world, including institutional problems such as inequities in the employment of women and minorities, faculty concerns such as balancing obligations to students and pressures to do research, and student problems such as forming responsible relationships. The pastoral frames its response in terms of an ideal academic community in which high ethical standards are maintained, all persons are treated with dignity, and the significant ethical questions are discussed. Specifically, the letter calls for the development of informed critical thinking on these questions through open forums and courses on the ethical questions that arise in all the major disciplines. The document insists that the whole academic environment should support the quest for the life of moral wisdom.

The proposals in the pastoral on this topic are broader and more pointed than we find in other reports, although "Integrity in the College Curriculum" has a helpful historical sketch on the rise of value-free education and a telling reminder that all courses can nurture the capacity for informed moral discourse. In this section, the bishops are on familiar ground as they call on colleges and universities to play their proper role of cultivating informed critical thinking on ethical issues.

SOCIAL RESPONSIBILITY

The bishops' document notes the complex questions that arise as institutions of higher learning carry out their role of public service. In response, the letter envisions colleges and universities fighting the excessive individualism in our culture and educating future leaders who will work for justice, human rights, and the common good. It poses this challenge: "For the college or university to be an authentic teacher of social justice, it must conduct its own affairs in a just way."[12] In this regard, the letter calls for "a prudent policy of preferential admission of minority students," and supports the effort to hire more women and minority faculty members as a matter of justice and as a means of enriching the faculty. Colleges and universities need a moral vision to sustain and focus their efforts, to meet their social responsibilities, and to promote the communal life of wisdom.

The pastoral letter thus contains an explicit prophetic dimension that lies outside the intention of the other three reports. It is crucial that the struggle for social justice be included in the public debate on higher education and the pastoral helps move us in that direction.

In this first draft the bishops have entered the public debate on higher education as a dialogue partner, much as they have done in the pastorals on peace and the economy. They do not claim any definitive answers but offer their perspectives and insights for consideration. In the first part of the document, they present their visions and strategies, mindful of the dignity of individuals and the social character of human existence. An essential aspect of their response to the concerns of higher education comes in the second part of the letter in which they stress the importance of the formation of faith communities on campuses. Their crucial thoughts in developing leaders, personal growth, religious knowledge, and social justice cannot be developed here.

The pastoral letter has a broader intention and covers more ground than the other three reports. It places individual questions in larger contexts. It stands as a reminder to the academic community that education is a concern of all citizens and that the problems of higher education cannot be solved in isolation. It raises questions of perspective, principles, morality, and social justice that can easily be overlooked in the public debate. It acknowledges the great contributions of

POPE FRANCIS AND CAMPUS MINISTRY

higher education and the ways that the church is enriched by its association with the academic world.

The pastoral letter is not a complete treatise on higher education. It is a document on campus ministry. However, the letter understands campus ministry as occurring "wherever the concerns of the church and higher education intersect." The document intends to address all those who care about our institutions of higher education, both public and private. It asks for a new partnership between church and higher education in the quest for the life of wisdom.

DIALOGUE WITH FRANCIS

As his visit to the United States made clear, Pope Francis has excellent pastoral instincts and skills. We can gain a better understanding of Francis as a pastor by examining two of his fundamental convictions: The Holy Spirit is at work in the whole church and all its members; and Christ is the model for all pastoral ministry. Jorge Bergoglio gave an initial indication of his pastoral style when he was first introduced to the vast throng assembled in St. Peter's Square and broke tradition by asking the people to do him the favor of praying for him. Dressed simply, he bowed his head as the huge crowd grew silent and prayed for the new pope. Witnessed by millions of people through live television and frequent replays, this powerful symbolic gesture revealed the pastoral heart of Pope Francis and set the tone for his ministry as Bishop of Rome. Since that initial iconic moment, Pope Francis has acted as a pastor who recognizes the presence of the Holy Spirit in the church and appreciates the spiritual bonds he shares with the people he serves. We can gain a deeper appreciation of the significance of the pope's pastoral style by recalling the broad history of ministry in the church.

In the early years of the Jesus movement, there was a powerful sense that all the baptized had special gifts of the Spirit that were to be used to build up the Body of Christ and serve the common good. The whole baptismal community, animated by the Spirit, was responsible for keeping alive the memory of Jesus and furthering his mission in the world. All the members shared in the royal priesthood of Christ. The pastoral leaders charged with overseeing the community were admonished "not to quench the Spirit" and not to lord it over the other members. Rather, they had the task of serving the community by encouraging and coordinating the spiritual gifts of all the members.

Some scholars see the history of ordained ministry in the church as a gradual process of clericalization, which created a privileged caste in the church by placing the diverse functions originally shared by all the baptized into the hands of the bishops and the clergy assisting them. After the time of Constantine (d. 337), senior clergy began to adopt imperial trappings and to assume more authority over other members of the church. Theological developments in the Middle Ages laid the groundwork for viewing priests as "other Christs" and identifying the church with the hierarchy.

Vatican II challenged this clericalization of the church, in part, by retrieving the earlier emphasis on the Holy Spirit, "who dwells in the church and in the hearts of the faithful." After extensive debates and various revisions, the Council produced the *Dogmatic Constitution on the Church* (*Lumen gentium*), which treated the "People of God" in chapter two before discussing the "Hierarchical Structure of the Church" in chapter three.[13] This carefully chosen sequence, which starts with the assumption that the Spirit is active in all the members of the church, set the fundamental framework for the conciliar teaching on pastoral ministry as service to the community. Through baptism, all the faithful share in the priesthood of Christ and the gifts of the Holy Spirit. They participate in the mission of the church not by the delegation of the hierarchy, but by virtue of their baptism. All the baptized, animated by the Spirit, are called to holiness and are co-responsible for the well-being of the faith community. The task of the ordained leaders is to "uncover with a sense of faith, acknowledge with joy and foster with diligence the various humble and exalted charisms of the laity."[14] A theology of the Holy Spirit grounds a collaborative style of church leadership that promotes dialogue and respects the instinctive gifts of the faithful. The church is the whole people of God and cannot be identified with the pope and bishops. In these ways and others, Vatican II set the stage for a process of declericalization and a reform of pastoral ministry. Much of the thrust of this process, however, was blunted by Pope John Paul II, who put his own personal stamp on pastoral ministry due to his remarkable charismatic gifts, and by Pope Benedict, who encouraged "the reform of the reform" movement and seemed to delight in the trappings of the papal office.

And now, Pope Francis, who has long embraced the pastoral thrust of Vatican II, has reenergized the spirit of the Council. His consistent efforts to disavow the privileges and trappings of high church office have become familiar to a broad audience within church circles and beyond: living in a small apartment where he cooked his own meals and using public transportation while serving as cardinal-archbishop of Buenos Aires; now as pope living in the Vatican guest house instead of the papal palace and wearing simple papal garb and liturgical vestments.

The simple lifestyle of Francis is rooted in his deep spiritual convictions. This becomes clearer when we consider his daily prayer routine: praying the Liturgy of the Hours from the breviary in the morning; celebrating the Eucharist; saying the Rosary; spending an hour of adoration before the Blessed Sacrament; and finding brief moments for prayer throughout the day. The pastoral style consistently practiced by Francis seems even more inspiring when considered in the context of his spiritual regimen.

In tune with the pastoral thrust of Vatican II, Pope Francis has appropriated the conciliar image of the church as the people of God. He speaks admiringly of the "holy, faithful people of God," who are on a Spirit-inspired "journey through history, with joys and sorrows."[15] He highlights the conciliar teaching that "all the faithful, considered as a whole, are infallible in matters of belief."[16] Commenting on Mary of Nazareth, the pope insists: "If you want to know who she is you ask theologians; if you want to know how to love her you have to ask the people." He is taken with the holiness of ordinary people who are raising children and earning a living, and has expressed admiration for his loving grandmother, Rosa, who "suffered so much" and still "always went forward with courage." Francis, much like his great predecessor, John XXIII, sees himself as a pastor who walks with the people of God on the journey of life, reminding them that the merciful and forgiving God accompanies every individual on the journey. When the newly elected Pope asked for prayers, he was giving expression to his deep pastoral conviction that he is in a Spirit-filled relationship with all the people he serves, a relationship that is enriched by mutual prayer and collaborative ministry.

The pastoral instincts of Pope Francis are not only animated by the Holy Spirit, but also are formed by the example of Jesus. In another richly symbolic and well-publicized event, the Pope celebrated Mass on Holy Thursday at a juvenile detention center on the outskirts of Rome. Recalling the actions of Jesus at the Last Supper, he washed and kissed the feet of twelve young people, including a Muslim girl. He told them this was a sign that "I am at your service," adding that Jesus teaches us to "help one another."

The pastoral sensitivities of the first Jesuit Pope are heavily influenced by the *Spiritual Exercises of St. Ignatius of Loyola*, who advocated imaginative meditation on the concrete life of the historical Jesus. Traditionally, Jesus is portrayed as priest, prophet, and king or shepherd. It is the shepherd image that has captured the imagination of Francis. Jesus is the Good Shepherd who knows his sheep and guides them, always ready to rescue the strays. The sheep recognize his voice and follow him. The Gospels portray Jesus as a community builder. At his baptism, he identifies himself with the mission of John the Baptist to reform the community of Israel. Jesus chose the Twelve, drawn from different regions and factions within Judaism, to symbolize his desire to restore Israel as a genuine light to the nations. His healing miracles, cleansing the ostracized lepers, for example, proclaimed in action that no one is excluded from the reign of God. Jesus reached out to the outcasts. He went to the house of Zacchaeus, the despised chief tax collector, and shared a meal with him. He broke social taboos by engaging the Samaritan woman in deep spiritual conversation and by inviting women to accompany him on his missionary journeys. Jesus had special concern for the poor in his society, no doubt influenced by his own experience as a Galilean peasant burdened by Roman taxation.

In word and action, Francis has committed himself to following the pastoral style and message of Jesus. He has criticized the pastoral approaches that obscure the primacy of the compassionate message of Christ, as when pastors are "obsessed with the transmission of a disjointed multitude of doctrines to be imposed insistently" and "insist only on issues related to abortion, gay marriage and the use of contraceptive methods."[17] The moral teaching of the church should be presented in the context of "the proclamation of the saving love of God," otherwise, "the moral edifice of the church is likely to fall like a house of cards, losing the freshness and fragrance of the Gospel."[18] Warning against preaching that is excessively moralistic, the pope admonishes preachers to proclaim and explain the central gospel message of divine mercy before drawing moral consequences. He wants more homilies directed to the problem of poverty and fewer to sexual sins.

Echoing the advice of Pope St. Gregory the Great (d. 604) in his very influential book *Pastoral Care*, Francis encourages pastors to follow the example of Christ, the Good Shepherd, and reach out to those in need of understanding, forgiveness, and mercy. The pope has set a good example of this pastoral approach by his loving, nonjudgmental attitude toward gay persons who are always embraced by God's unconditional love and by his welcoming approach to single mothers who bring their babies for baptism. The people of God, according to Francis, do not want clergy who act like bureaucrats, but courageous pastors who "walk through the dark night with them," without getting lost. Pastors must "accompany the flock that has a flair for finding new paths," without leaving anyone behind. Pastoral ministry, as envisioned and practiced by Francis, has clear Christ-like characteristics, including loving service, inclusive compassion, and ultimate hope.

Consultation is a key component of the leadership style of Pope Francis. He has insisted that church leaders listen carefully to the "beat of this age." The church gains credibility by paying attention to how people are living their daily lives, with their "sadness and distress" and their "joys and hopes." In preparation for the 2014–15 synod meetings on family life, Francis asked the national conferences of bishops to conduct wide-ranging consultations to learn what Catholics feel and think about difficult family issues. The pope hoped that this practice would help the synod deal with facts more than abstract ideas, so that the church would find more effective ways of ministering to families. Francis is convinced that wide consultation leads to better pastoral practices. He learned this from experience, admitting that as a young superior he made mistakes by acting quickly without adequate consultation. As pope, he has adapted a much more open, dialogical, and consultative approach to decision-making.

Viewed from the perspective of the pastoral practice of Pope Francis, "The Quest for Wisdom"—the draft of the initial effort to produce a campus ministry pastoral letter—had some positive features that can still be retrieved to enrich campus ministry today: making an effort to understand strengths and weaknesses of the academic world; engaging members of the university in dialogue; bringing the gospel message to bear on the challenges facing academe; learning to appreciate the contributions made by scholars to the common good; presenting the Christian message coherently; understanding the servant role of the church on campus; recognizing consultation as a valuable tool for improving pastoral ministry; reading the signs of the times as crucial to the mission of the church; identifying the core message of Christ and organizing pastoral practices around it; acting on the centrifugal thrust of the gospel; and modeling campus ministry on Jesus, the compassionate servant.

Campus ministers who retrieve "Quest" through Francis put great emphasis on learning from others: for example, students who can help them understand the joys and sorrows of collegiate life; faculty members who are experts in various fields of interest; administrators who can articulate the dreams and challenges of the university; coaches who know how to motivate young people; staff members who know the needs of students; and colleagues in ministry who have developed successful programs.

Faith communities on campus faithful to the style of Francis create an open atmosphere that invites all the members to participate as both teachers and learners and that encourages decision-makers to consult with those affected. Some examples include: a pastor wanting to make changes in the weekend Mass schedule provides a mechanism for all the members to voice their opinion; and the student cochairs of the social justice committee have an open discussion of a proposal for promoting racial harmony on campus. The Francis effect on campus ministry creates a community of faith dedicated to the broad consultation employed in the development of "The Quest for Wisdom."

2

THE DRAFT DOCUMENT

After nearly two years of working closely with the editorial committee, I produced a draft of the proposed pastoral entitled "The Quest for Wisdom: The Church in Dialogue with Higher Education." The theme was inspired by Pope John Paul II, who insisted that the university and the church share an interest in promoting wisdom. In composing the document, I was responding to various voices: the bishops who initiated the process; the individuals and groups who participated in the consultations; the faculty and students I served over many years; and the bishops and experienced campus ministers on the editorial committee. The resulting draft, completed in early 1985, gained approval from the bishops' Committee on Education and their Administrative Board. With these approvals in place and with the blessing of Bishop Friend, I presented the document to the bishops assembled in Collegeville for their meeting in June 1985. For reasons that were never entirely clear to me or the committee, the bishops voted to reject the proposed pastoral and gave the editorial committee the task of rewriting it, with a new deadline of November 1985 when they would be next meeting in Washington. My informal conversations with a few bishops led me to the unsubstantiated conjecture that several bishops, understandably, did not have time to read the document, and that a powerful cardinal who opposed it influenced others. What became clear was that the bishops wanted a less ambitious and more intramural pastoral that focused on the functions of the church on campus. I was aware of the weaknesses of "The Quest for Wisdom" in its effort to voice wisdom to the world of higher education, since a sophisticated discussion of reform was now underway among academics. Regardless, it seemed that a more intramural approach missed a great and welcome opportunity to address the concerns of higher education at a time when the bishops were courageously and insightfully addressing the issues of peace and war and economic justice. As the committee quickly began the rewriting process, my hope was to get as much of the outward thrust of the rejected document into the next draft.

"The Quest for Wisdom: The Church in Dialogue with Higher Education" was initially released as a draft for discussion on March 21, 1983. It was divided into two major parts: The Church in Dialogue with Higher Education; and the Church on Campus. Both parts were structured as a dialogue, with the church first listening and then responding. The uniting theme of the document is the common search for wisdom by both the university and the church. The proposed document was never published. The first part of the longer draft is published here for the first time with permission of the United States Conference of Catholic Bishops. It is not only of historical interest but can serve as a catalyst and a guide for campus ministry today as it continues the dialogue with higher education.

THE QUEST FOR WISDOM

GENERAL INTRODUCTION

The passionate search for the "life of wisdom," as Pope John Paul II has indicated, is at the center of the "deep bond that exists between the Church and the university."[1] In the ideal life of wisdom, human beings achieve a richer personal synthesis that is the fulfillment of the pursuit of truth; discover the highest principles that integrate all knowledge; and learn to combine the theoretical with the practical, self-fulfillment with a concern for the common good, and knowledge with the light of love. The church and higher education are natural partners in the quest for this kind of wisdom. Unfortunately, in the modern world both sides have failed at times to recognize and respect that bond. Through this pastoral letter, we hope to renew the dialogue and prepare for a new era of cooperation. We do so recognizing the proper autonomy of higher education and without any desire to dominate or dictate. Our desire is to work together for the welfare of individuals and society. As

Pope John Paul II stated: "If then there is not established ever more profoundly a bond between the Church and the university it is the human person who will be harmed as a result...nor will the culture be fully humanized."[2]

In our 1981 statement on Catholic higher education, we concluded by noting "the excellent intellectual and pastoral leadership of many Catholics engaged as teachers, administrators, and campus ministers in the colleges and universities which are not Catholic."[3] We said at that time that "we hope for a future opportunity to speak of their invaluable contribution to the intellectual life of our country."[4] In this pastoral letter, we are pleased to fulfill that hope and turn our attention to the ministry of the church on these public and private campuses where each year over four million Catholics, along with millions of others, are being prepared as future leaders of society and church.[5] As we examine this situation, we are mindful of our previous comments on the crucial importance of Catholic higher education. We noted the distinctive task of campus ministry on Catholic campuses to call the total institution to spread the gospel and to preserve and enrich its religious traditions.[6] In addition, we appreciate the suggestions for this document made by those who serve at Catholic colleges and universities. Our consultations remind us that all who minister in the world of higher education have certain common concerns and similar desires for cooperation. Thus, we believe that many of our perspectives and suggestions in this pastoral letter will be helpful to those who serve so well in our Catholic institutions of higher education.

In listening to campus ministers express their concerns and hopes, it is evident to us that their ministry is unavoidably connected with the whole situation of higher education in this country. In fact, we can say that campus ministry occurs wherever the concerns of the church and higher education intersect. While we realize that this does not provide us with a strict definition of campus ministry, it does give us a comprehensive way of examining a wide variety of ministerial activities on campus. The pastoral work of campus ministers involves them with persons whose lives are heavily influenced by the academic environment. Students are permanently affected both by the classroom and life on campus. Faculty members are engrossed in their own fields of interest and research. Administrators are concerned about the well-being of the institution. Everyone on campus encounters ethical and value questions raised by life in the academic world. Campus ministers simply cannot remain indifferent to this world. Fidelity to the gospel calls for an effort to renew academic life, especially since it affects the personal and collective lives of so many.[7] Good pastoral care demands that campus ministers respond to the human concerns generated by academic life.

For this reason, we address, in the first part of this pastoral letter, some of the current concerns of higher education that have the clearest relationship to the work of the church on campus. We enter into this discussion as a dialogue partner with all who recognize the crucial importance of higher education for the welfare of our society. We claim no easy answers but offer our vision and suggestions based on our traditional understanding of the dignity of the human person. We do so with profound respect for the freedom and autonomy of the academic community and after having listened carefully to numerous voices from colleges and universities.[8] It is gratifying that so many have encouraged us to contribute our comments and insights to the ongoing discussion.

In the second part of the letter, we turn to the specific concerns of the church on campus as we have heard them expressed in extensive consultation with campus ministers, students, and others. Drawing on the experience of many successful campus ministers, we respond by sketching out an ideal vision of the church on campus and by offering concrete proposals on how to make this vision real. In this second part, we are speaking from the perspective of our Christian faith and especially our understanding of the church as a community of faith that seeks and treasures the gift of wisdom.

THE CHURCH IN DIALOGUE WITH HIGHER EDUCATION

LISTENING

INTRODUCTION

After extensive consultation in the preparation of this document, certain common concerns emerged. In large measure, they reflect much of the recent scientific research on higher education in the United States.[9] As we consider this material, we are especially attuned to the issues that we can constructively address as advocates of human dignity and as moral teachers concerned about the common good. There is no doubt that higher education in the United States has made impressive contributions to the welfare of individuals and society. In our consultations, we have learned a great deal and have been enriched by the wealth of wisdom found in the academic community. However, there are also serious problems that impede the development of the full potential of higher education. In this "listening" section of the first part of this pastoral letter we will summarize some of these concerns. Then in the next section, we will respond to these problems of offering our vision of a direction for the future as well as some suggestions for moving toward the ideals embodied in this vision.

NATURE AND PURPOSE OF HIGHER EDUCATION

A key element in the current debate is the nature, purpose, and value of higher education.[10] The term "higher education" embraces a variety of public and private institutions, ranging from large research universities to small two-year colleges. Most of these institutions have undergone significant changes in the last two decades due to changing societal conditions. For the next few decades, increased competition for a shrinking pool of traditional-aged students will be a major factor in policy decisions. More nontraditional students are attending colleges and universities. There is more governmental regulation. These and other factors have produced a new debate on the nature and purpose of higher education. At the extremes, a few want to dismantle the entire system on the grounds that it is unavoidably oppressive, while others long to return to the classical elitist system. However, within the mainstream, there is still substantial agreement that higher education should collectively include teaching, research, and public service. Students should be challenged and enabled to sharpen their cognitive skills, to develop morally and emotionally, and to attain practical competency. Higher education should benefit society by preserving and advancing knowledge and by helping to solve common problems.[11] The main problem today is finding a proper balance among these laudable goals, setting priorities, and discovering a way to unify them. Individual institutions are searching for their precise purposes and the unique contributions they can make.

Many educators express concern that public confidence in higher education has been shaken. The fact that the financial rewards for going to college are not so obvious has raised further questions about its value. Some institutions, especially the less selective private schools, are worried about surviving because of declining enrollments and financial pressures. In these times of change and crisis, academic leaders are necessarily challenged to rethink the nature and purpose of higher education.

QUALITY

In our consultations, we heard many negative comments about the quality of higher education. Students complain about ill-prepared faculty members, unimaginative teaching methods, boring classes, and irrelevant curriculums. Faculty members speak of grade inflation, poorly prepared students, and reduced academic standards. Some admit that departmental pressures to publish and financial pressures to do outside consulting at times hurt their performance in the classroom. They are worried that they have a diminished voice in improving the quality of an educational system that is heavily influenced by the utilitarian and consumerist mentality in the culture. Administrators describe a variety of problems: declining enrollments and financial pressures make survival more important than the search for excellence; good faculty members are lost to the higher salaries of the corporate world; cuts in public funds reduce basic research; the tenured status of an aging faculty makes it difficult to find openings for younger, well-qualified teachers; and the whole precollegiate educational system fails to prepare many students adequately for higher education. Such often repeated criticisms find a good deal of support in the research data. For example, scores on the Scholastic Aptitude Tests given to high school seniors are much lower now than they were twenty years ago.[12]

However, positive comments were also heard in our consultations. Students praised caring professors, the intellectual stimulation on campus, and innovative classes. Individual faculty members claimed their research and consulting work improved their classroom teaching. Administrators spoke of the overall strength of our system of higher education compared to other countries and reminded us that alumni often report general satisfaction with their collegiate education. Efforts to improve the quality of education are in place. For example, over 80 percent of colleges and universities have instituted comprehensive basic skills programs. Research indicates that cognitive development does take place in collegiate years as students become more open-minded and improve their ability to think critically.[13]

Thus, there is a degree of ambivalence on the question of quality. However, despite the positive indications, the dominant sentiment we heard from the academic community was one of great concern about the quality of higher education.

BALANCE

Closely linked to the issue of quality is that of achieving a proper balance among the various goals of higher education. Many claim that, in general, there is currently an overemphasis on practical competency or vocational training to the great detriment of the cognitive goals of developing critical thinking and a cultivated mind. Since many students are in school to get a degree in order to get a better job, they choose schools, majors, and courses accordingly. Career-oriented majors require specialized classes that leave little time for general education. Institutions of higher learning are forced to respond to these demands in a variety of ways. Thus, courses in business, engineering, computer science, and other professions are expanding while the humanities, social sciences, and fine arts are declining. The trend, no doubt, reflects tough economic times but also may be associated with a utilitarian, anti-intellectual strain in our culture.

A further imbalance occurs when cognitive learning focuses almost exclusively on the empirical methods of the natural sciences and neglects the broader approaches associated with the liberal arts. It is of special concern to us that despite an increase in the number of religious studies programs, there are still so few courses taught about religion in many institutions. As a result, society suffers because most college graduates have a meager knowledge of the world's great religious traditions and especially the Judeo-Christian tradition, which has helped shape our Western culture. Of course, this description of imbalance, which reflects general statistical data, should not obscure the fact that some liberal arts and church-related institutions have maintained a more integrated approach to undergraduate education. However, it remains true that higher education is generally slanted toward the empirical and the vocational. This, in turn, undercuts the traditional goal of producing the wise person who can think critically and view problems in a broad perspective.

VALUES AND ETHICS

Many people in higher education are concerned about values and ethics. Warnings are heard about institutional problems such as the failure to deal with ethical issues in professional schools and career-oriented programs, grade inflation that cheapens education, the danger of losing academic freedom in the face of external funding, questionable recruiting practices fostered by declining enrollments, unhealthy alliances with the military-industrial complex, the deterioration of a sense of community on campuses, inequities in the employment of women and minorities, and unfair practices in the recruitment and treatment of athletes. Ethical questions also arise in relation to the faculty: How should teachers relate to students in an ethical way, combine objectivity and personal enthusiasm in classroom teaching, balance obligations to students and the pressure to do research, maintain integrity and freedom while accepting external funding, combat unfair tenure practices, maintain civility and fairness in professional relationships, deal with cheating, and contribute to the well-being of society?

Student life inevitably raises questions about sexual problems, drinking and drugs, cheating, personal relationships, career decisions, social responsibility, as well as ethical issues connected with class material.

Fortunately, there is a brighter side to this picture. Evidence suggests that during collegiate years, students learn to be more tolerant and open to diverse groups of people.[14] More courses on professional ethics are being offered. Religious interest is not extinguished by attending college as some suppose. For example, college alumni attend church services at least as frequently as those who did not attend college.[15] Collegiate years offer a great opportunity for students to discover their talents, values, and aspirations and to move toward greater personal maturity. However, despite these positive points there remains a general perception that institutions of higher learning should be doing more in this area. Questions of values and ethics are too often ignored, both in the classroom and in the life of the college or university.

SOCIAL RESPONSIBILITY

In the United States, public service has come to be recognized as a responsibility of higher education. In the modern world, meeting this responsibility involves complex questions. For example, how actively should colleges and universities respond to racial problems, economic difficulties, international problems, the women's movement, world hunger, and the nuclear threat?[16] A wide range of options exist. Some persons support a very indirect involvement through strictly academic means while others expect higher education to help shape a bitter society through boycotts, stock divestitures, and direct political action. Between these extremes, many advocate a more measured response to selected issues through the traditional academic means of teaching, research, and technical assistance. As a matter of fact, most colleges and universities are increasingly involved in social issues through research institutes, faculty consultation, international assistance programs, and student internships. Community colleges often play an important role in local issues. Research suggests that college graduates tend to be more socially involved and politically active than those who did not attend college.[17] Higher education unavoidably influences the thought patterns of those who help shape the social order. The question is how wisely and to what ends this influence is exerted.

The way that higher education conducts its own internal affairs also has an influence on social questions. A key issue in this regard is that of access. Our national ideal is equal educational opportunity for all citizens so that they can develop their potential fully. It is often claimed that we have the most open system of higher education in the world. The growth of community college students identifying themselves as belonging to an ethnic minority has increased substantially since 1973.[18] Despite these gains, ethnic minorities are still underrepresented among college students. For example, only 13 percent of all black eighteen-year-olds entered college in 1983 as compared to 24 percent for all students.[19] In addition, there are many who fear that we will move to a more elitist system as financial difficulties increase and admission standards are raised.

Faculty hiring is another issue with obvious social ramifications. Currently blacks, Hispanics, American Indians and women are underrepresented on college faculties.[20] The Federal Government has indicated that institutions should set their own goals for hiring more minorities and women. Various plans have been adopted to improve this situation. However, administrators agree that even with goodwill and planning, which includes vigorous recruitment, it is difficult to make progress. While some favor preferential hiring, others argue that faculty members must be hired strictly based on merit in order to provide the highest quality education possible.

Many other concerns were heard during our consultations, including questions of governance and specific financial problems. We have highlighted the ones that seem to be of common concern to both the church and higher education.

RESPONDING

In our consultations, we were pleased that so many welcomed a word from church leaders on these issues. This seems fitting when we consider the historical role of the church as a founder and supporter of higher education. Thus, we offer, in the spirit of dialogue, our perspectives on these concerns, as well as some more specific suggestions.

THE DIGNITY OF PERSONS

Our starting point is the nature and dignity of all human beings who have within themselves "an ultimate meaning upon which depends both the values of personal existence and of life in society."[21] We human beings are "the center and crown" of all things on earth.[22] We are unique and unrepeatable individuals called and identified by our own name, involved in a personal quest for the infinite.[23] At the same time, we are social beings who must relate to others in order to develop our potential.[24] We are creatures who know our limitations in a variety of ways, and yet we feel ourselves to be boundless in our longings and summoned to a higher life.[25] We sense a division within ourselves and "as a result, all of human life, whether individual or collective, shows itself to be a dramatic struggle between good and evil, between light and darkness."[26] We are unified creatures who live a bodily existence as well as a spiritual life in which we transcend the "whole sum of mere things."[27] In our "most secret core and sanctuary," we all know the call of conscience to search for the truth and to work for genuine solutions to life's problems.[28] As human beings, we can direct ourselves toward truth and goodness only through free choice that is personally motivated and does not result from blind impulse or mere external pressure.[29] We are able to transcend our selfishness and enter into loving relationships; but our hearts always long for a love that is imperishable. Our dignity is also manifested in the search for truth that brings scientific progress and a more penetrating understanding of our intelligible but ultimately mysterious world.[30] The search for truth finds its perfection in the life of wisdom, "for wisdom gently attracts the mind...to a quest and a love for what is true and good."[31] It is wisdom that enables us to pass "through visible realities to those which are unseen."[32] True wisdom enlarges our vision and can never be the monopoly of any particular elite group. Wisdom adds meaning and purpose to the progress of science and integrates all the knowledge we can acquire. For Christian believers, Jesus Christ is the greatest example of the life of wisdom and thus embodies the highest aspirations of the whole human family.

Our understanding of human existence is well-summarized in this notion of the "life of wisdom." Church and university have traditionally been dedicated to that ideal. We think it can still draw people of goodwill together in search of answers to the common concerns of higher education.

WISDOM AND THE NATURE AND PURPOSE OF HIGHER EDUCATION

It is crucial that the dignity and worth of human beings be kept in the center of our reflections on the nature, purpose, and value of higher education. Education can be thought of as the entire process by which persons are "assisted in the harmonious development of their physical, moral, and intellectual endowments."[33] It aims to form individuals who are moving, with a deep sense of ultimate purpose, toward greater freedom, maturity, and integration. At the same time, genuine education includes a sense of responsibility for the common good and provides skills for active involvement in community life.[34] In short, education is a vital means for personal and social development.

Family life remains central in this process. As Pope John Paul II said, "The family is the first and fundamental school of social living."[35] Although the family is primary, it is not the only educating community. Schools make their unique contribution by cultivating the intellect, improving judgment, passing on the cultural heritage, promoting constructive values, and preparing for professional and family life.[36] Institutions of higher learning further this process by attending to their primary purpose, which is "the passionate and disinterested search for truth" that makes human beings free and helps them achieve their full humanity in accord with their dignity and worth.[37] In addition, their educational commitment should extend to enabling students to deal with ethical issues and to achieve a harmonious integration of all aspects of their lives.[38] Higher education has the task "to lead the mind to truth, so that it will not succumb to the deadly infection of relativism; to lead the will to the good by rescuing it from an empty and dead-end anarchism; to convert the entire person to the objectivity of values, in opposition to every form of subjectivism."[39] In other words, colleges and universities have the task of preparing individuals for the life of wisdom in which truth and goodness are integrated into a higher synthesis. The broad goal of preparing for a life of wisdom and virtue provides a context within which we can more clearly define the specific goals of sharpening cognitive skills, developing the moral and affective life, and imparting practical competency. Each institution can work this out in detail in accord with its own history, tradition, specific character, and current situation. There are many paths leading to the life of wisdom.

Higher education is valuable because it releases human potential, helps shape a better future, and contributes to the common good. It "can help elevate the human family to a better understanding of truth, goodness and beauty and the formation of judgments, which can embody universal values."[40] College is not for everyone. However, everyone who is qualified should be given the opportunity and encouragement to attend college. We support our system of higher education in the United States, both public and private, in all its diversity. We encourage public support for our colleges and universities so that they can make even greater contributions to the good of society and the pursuit of the life of wisdom.

WISDOM AND QUALITY

When we consider the quality of higher education, our general perspective reminds us that commitment to the full development of students toward the life of wisdom must be a major concern. Students are not just commodities but persons with potentials to be discovered and developed. This principle should be kept in mind as trustees assume greater responsibility for long-term development and healthy systemic change, as administrators make decisions about methods to attract new students, and as faculty members work on their professional development and divide their time between research and teaching. The concern for students should motivate the public to demand adequate governmental funding for higher education. In this regard, we support the Carnegie Council's contention that the states that have done well in support of public education "need now to render substantial aid also to private higher education wherever they have not already done so."[41]

It is our conviction that a vigorous private system that offers healthy competition to the public system will help achieve better education for all students. We also agree with the Carnegie Council's suggestion that a system of granting tuition scholarships based on need to students be instituted so that the recipients can choose which college or university they wish to attend.[42] This is one way of promoting healthy competition and improving the quality of education. Government can also help by giving more support for basic research while respecting academic freedom and limiting unnecessary regulations.

Students themselves can greatly improve the quality of education by taking greater responsibility for their own learning, seeking out close relationships with professors, taking greater part in extracurricular, academic, and cultural opportunities on campus, and by interacting more with students from various backgrounds and cultures.

Higher education can be improved only as part of an overall plan that affects society and touches all levels of education. Such a plan should include efforts by various institutions to raise the standard of living of the poor, to improve the quality of family life, to find ways to motivate apathetic students, to overcome a lingering anti-intellectualism in the country, to secure adequate funding for all education, to offer better salaries to teachers, to insist on higher standards in primary and secondary schools, and to reward professors for good teaching. Even such a partial listing reminds us of the difficulty of the task: there are no simple formulas for achieving progress.

The call for improvement should not blind us to the positive achievements of our education system, nor the skill and dedication of so many good teachers and administrators. The life of wisdom is always an ideal that exceeds our grasp. However, movement toward this ideal is worthy of our best efforts.

WISDOM AND BALANCE

As we consider the question of balance in higher education, it is crucial to keep alive the traditional vision of an authentic liberal education. Such an education inculcates a habit of mind that enables persons to think critically and to immerse themselves in lifelong learning. As Cardinal Newman reminds us, it gives individuals the ability to synthesize by "viewing many things at once as a whole, of referring them severally to their true place in the universal system, of understanding their respective values and determining their mutual independence."[43] The ideal is a disciplined intellect, "which has learned to leaven the dense mass of facts and events with the elastic force of reason."[44] A liberal education leads to "the harmonious integration of the various internal powers in which human nature abounds (the will, the affectivity, instincts, etc.) in a higher equilibrium under the headship of the personal ego."[45] In short, liberal education aims at acquiring wisdom that provides perspective, integration, balance, and a lifelong love of learning.

A complete liberal education includes study about religion. This means learning the history, teachings, and practices of the various world religions, especially of the Judeo-Christian tradition that has shaped Western civilization and our own culture in particular. It also means that the religious aspects of various other disciplines such as literature, history, and art be treated in courses in these areas. Teaching about religion should be done by qualified professors, in accord with academic standards of objectivity and by making use of the best methods of scholarship. The classroom is not the place for evangelizing or proselytizing. In private as well as in public institutions, professors teaching theology classes are well advised to strive for a similar objectivity and to maintain rigorous academic standards.

Colleges and universities have a duty to teach about religion because religious knowledge has an inherent value, constitutes a legitimate academic discipline, is part of our cultural heritage, can broaden understanding and tolerance of others' values, and can serve as an integrating principle for the rest of learning. Students have a right to know about religion because it is essential for understanding themselves and the world. For example, consider the obvious influence of religion on international relationships, national identity, cultural development, family life, and personal value systems. As Newman said, "A truly liberating and elevating education is incomplete without the study of theology and religion"[46] because religious truth is "not only a portion but a condition of general knowledge."[47] The life of wisdom needs the focus and breadth that comes from religious knowledge.

We hope this vision of genuine liberal education will be kept in mind as institutions of higher learning work on achieving a healthy balance among their cognitive, affective, and practical goals. This suggests a great variety of institutional responses: to establish a department of religious studies, to provide more funds for effective programs in the humanities and the fine arts, to put more effort into strengthening general education, to work out an effective core curriculum, to teach the sciences in a way that creates a sense of awe and wonder, to keep graduate programs in the liberal arts alive, to create an atmosphere in which genuine learning is prized, to establish programs in liberal studies for adult learners, to form more interdisciplinary classes, to stay alert to the possibility that interest in the humanities may increase, and to assist liberal arts graduates in finding jobs.

Faculty members can assist greatly in redressing current imbalances in many ways: by working together on interdisciplinary courses; by encouraging their students to more precise thinking; by inculcating a love of learning; by fighting for traditional academic values; and by treating any appropriate religious aspects of their course materials objectively and fairly.

Amid harsh economic realities and the many pressures of collegiate life, students should accept the challenge to develop their intellectual powers, to enter the great quest for truth, and to prepare for lifelong learning. We commend those institutions that have maintained a healthy balance in their curricula and programs, thereby enabling their students to become well-rounded individuals. We admire administrators, faculty members, and students who have struggled against great societal pressures to keep the tradition of liberal education alive. Our society needs persons of wisdom who possess cultivated minds and good hearts placed at the service of the larger community. Higher education faces a great and crucial challenge in helping to form such wise individuals.

WISDOM, VALUES, AND ETHICS

When the total well-being of students is placed at the center of our thinking, the responsibility of higher education to attend explicitly to questions of values and ethics becomes clearer. College students are in the process of developing morally and of forming their value systems that will sustain them in their careers and personal lives. They face many ethical problems that arise in their personal lives and in their courses of study. They must work out their relationships with family, church, and society. They need guidance, role models, and a supportive community.

Let us envision the kind of ideal academic community they need.

It is a moral community in which high ethical standards are maintained. For instance, women and minorities are treated justly, departments work in harmony, public service is performed, proper provision is made for the handicapped, and athletic programs are run honestly with the total welfare of the athletes in mind.

It is a learning community in which academic freedom is maintained despite governmental and corporate funding for research, the right to education commensurate with a person's capabilities is maintained, academic standards are kept high despite the competition to increase enrollments, the great ethical questions of the day are openly discussed, and courses in applied ethics are available that teach traditional wisdom and encourage critical thinking and open discussion.

It is a personal community in which all members are treated with dignity and the privacy of individuals is respected, administrators are concerned with the quality of campus life, faculty members are generous with their time and take a personal interest in their students. In such an ideal academic setting, students learn to respect others and to care about the common good. They gain knowledge of the great religious and moral traditions and learn to think critically about ethical matters. They can develop the traditional moral virtues of prudence, justice, fortitude, and temperance as well as public virtues that lead to responsible citizenship and service to society as a whole. They can grow gradually into mature adults with living examples to guide them. In short, the whole academic environment supports their quest for the life of moral wisdom.

To describe such an ideal academic community reminds us of all the individuals who have worked hard to put elements of this vision into practice. It also sets the agenda for renewed efforts by the campus community to move toward these high ethical standards. In this process, the limited role of higher education should be kept in mind. The moral development of students is, of course, influenced by family, church, and the culture. Colleges and universities make their unique contribution to this development by creating a healthy moral climate on campus and by encouraging informed critical thinking on questions of values and ethics. Complex ethical questions surround the topics of peace and war, respect for human life, genetic engineering, economic systems, world hunger, the rights of women and minorities, family life, the problems of the handicapped, the penal system, capital punishment, sexuality, and many others. These questions should be treated in the classroom and in open forums. Each discipline produces its own set of ethical questions that deserve explicit treatment. Thus, there is a need for courses in ethics not only in obvious areas such as medicine, law, and philosophy, but also in the fields of business and the physical and social sciences. Higher education, by teaching students to think clearly about questions of values and ethics, can make an important contribution to raising the level of moral discourse in our society.

WISDOM AND SOCIAL RESPONSIBILITY

From the perspective of our understanding of the communal nature of human existence, we are pleased that higher education in the United States has assumed public service as one of its tasks. This is especially important in our time when an excessive individualism that disregards the common good poses a deep threat to the well-being of our whole society. We envision colleges and universities educating leaders who will work for justice and human rights, engaging in research that will help alleviate human suffering, and producing graduates who are concerned citizens. Higher education can provide expert advice and technical assistance to public officials and can respond prudently with scholarly expertise to requests from other countries for assistance. It can mobilize resources to fight against such social problems as racism, sexism, consumerism, and excessive individualism, as well as the devaluing of human life and the threat of nuclear war.

The social responsibility of higher education also extends to its own internal life. As we have stated before, "For the college or university to be an authentic teacher of social justice, it must conduct its own affairs in a just way."[48] While the ideal of a socially conscious and just institution is clear, we recognize the great complexity involved in achieving it. In this regard, we support our national ideal of equal access for all. We see this as an important right for all students who can benefit from higher education.[49] Colleges and universities bear the responsibility, along with churches and other institutions, of trying to better the lot of disadvantaged persons. We support a prudent policy of preferential admission of minority students. Those responsible for decisions about admissions should consider the individual student's academic performance as well as his or her potential for benefiting from the collegiate experience and for contributing to society. We base our support for such a policy on the fact that prior grades and the results of standardized entrance tests are limited instruments for determining student potential and actual achievement. It is our hope that the admission of more minority students will enrich the academic community and will in the long run promote racial equality. Adequate funding must be available for students who cannot afford to go to college. We need government-funded tuition scholarships for those who are in need. We ask private funding agencies to consider the great societal advantages that occur when poor persons have the opportunity for further education. Disadvantaged students need precollege programs to prepare them for a new challenge. Once on campus, they need support and specific help so they can take full advantage of the opportunity. Balancing equality of access and the search for academic excellence is a difficult and complex task that calls for the best efforts of all concerned.

Community colleges especially deserve credit for their fine work in offering remedial classes and comprehensive programs. We encourage them to continue and to improve this effort. Equal access will do no good if disadvantaged students are not motivated to seize the opportunity. Parents, friends, relatives, clergy, coaches, and other influential persons should keep reminding youngsters of the importance of getting a good education. Students, for their own part, must come to understand that, ultimately, they bear the responsibility for their own learning.

We support the efforts of colleges and universities to hire women and minorities. At the same time, we realize that even with goodwill and effort, equitable levels may not be reached in the near future. However, it is a matter of justice that this effort be continued. Even partial success will enrich the faculty. The fact that women are paid less than men with comparable positions, credentials, and achievements is an example of the injustice borne by women in our society. The church and higher education must work together with others to eradicate all such inequities.

As human beings increasingly sense their essential interdependence, the advantages of bringing an international dimension to higher education become more apparent. Students who come to our colleges and universities from other lands bring an enriching diversity to our campuses. They must be treated with dignity, and their spiritual and cultural values must be respected. They, in turn, should try to understand our customs and to abide by our academic standards. The international exchange of students and faculty members can be a helpful method of building bridges between nations and of promoting world peace. The presence of foreign students is a visible reminder of the advantage of bringing a multicultural dimension to academic life in general.

We think that a moral vision is needed to sustain and focus the efforts of institutions of higher education to meet their social responsibilities. Human beings are individuals of intrinsic worth who are at the same time members of the great human family. They have individual rights and social responsibilities. In setting policy, institutions of higher learning must respect human dignity and foster a sense of commitment to the common good. Promoting the life of wisdom in this way is the noble duty and responsibility of colleges and universities.

There are, of course, no simple answers to these five complex issues, and we claim none. They can be separated for analysis, but in reality, they mutually influence one another. They are widely debated by professional educators, but we have observed no coherent and compelling vision to guide the discussion. The essence of our contribution is to insist that the notion of the dignity and nature of the human person must be moved to the center of the debate. We think that this crucial change will have a positive effect on both policy and practice in higher education. We used the traditional ideal of wisdom as one way of achieving perspective on the key issues. Our concrete suggestions are reflections of the best current efforts and constitute an invitation to search for more creative solutions. The lure of wisdom can draw higher education into a brighter future.

Vision and Summary

Each institution of higher learning must deal with these issues according to its own unique self-understanding.[50] Ideally, every college and university should have a dominant vision that gives it a sense of identity, direction, and purpose. This vision is developed out of the historical traditions of the institution and reflects the current experience of its members and its situation in the community. This ideal self-understanding guides the major decisions of the institution; energizes the cooperative efforts of faculty, students, and administrators; and integrates the knowledge acquired in the various intellectual disciplines. It provides a sense of stability and structures the effort to be of service to the larger community. The vision gives a human face to the campus community and engenders a spirit of loyalty and a commitment to self-sacrifice for the common good. From the perspective of the dominant vision, the institution refines its nature and purpose, improves the quality of its instruction, achieves a balance among its cognitive, affective, and practical goals, establishes its ethical standards, and responds to the cries for justice in the world.

Our consultations convince us that it is precisely such an operative vision that is lacking in many institutions of higher learning. We realize that this is related to larger societal problems and that some institutions have maintained or developed a healthy self-understanding. However, we encourage colleges and universities to undertake a self-examination that concentrates on the problem of creating and implementing a vision that will provide direction, purpose, and a sense of identity. In our view, the pursuit of the life of wisdom will inspire such a dominant vision. It has the advantage of providing a corrective to the economically motivated plans that currently dominate the decision-making in many colleges and universities. Such a vision, based on the theme of wisdom, will have to be worked out in detail and must respect the autonomy and uniqueness of each institution. In the first part of this pastoral letter, we have offered our perspectives and suggestions in the hope of promoting dialogue and constructive action that will lead to definite improvements in our colleges and universities. We remain convinced that higher education has great untapped potential to help create a better future for individuals and society.

DIALOGUE WITH FRANCIS

The positive outlook of Pope Francis on Christian discipleship comes into sharper focus when contrasted with the somber approach of the Catholic culture warriors in the United States, who emphasize the current warfare between faithful Christians and secular society. In 2014, Robert George, a professor of law at Princeton, who is widely considered to have major influence on prominent American bishops, gave a talk at the annual National Catholic Prayer Breakfast, portraying the battle lines in the culture wars. According to Professor George, mainstream American culture finds acceptable only "tame Catholics," who do not embrace the totality of church teaching and are "ashamed of the gospel." The American "love affair with Jesus and his Church is over," making our culture more hostile to religion. The church in the

United States is now in a "Good Friday" situation, which means: "The days of socially acceptable Christianity are over. The days of comfortable Catholicism are past." Today, Christians who are faithful witnesses to the gospel risk "the scorn and reproach" of "polite society." Faithful Christians place in jeopardy important personal values, including opportunities for employment and professional advancement, recognition and honors, even treasured friendships and family harmony.

According to Professor George, the two major battles in the culture war are over abortion and gay marriage. A Catholic who opposes gay marriage is seen by the secular culture as "a homophobe, a bigot, someone who doesn't believe in equality." While tamed Catholics who are "ashamed of the gospel" are socially acceptable in the United States, faithful Catholics who oppose abortion and gay marriage pay a "heavy price" for taking up the cross. We get a sense of this dire outlook in the comment of the late Cardinal Francis George of Chicago to the effect that he expected to die in bed, but his immediate successor will die in prison and the next in line will die a martyr in the public arena.

Robert George attracts attention because, as Archbishop John Myers of Newark has noted, many bishops rely on him as "a touchstone" and "the pre-eminent Catholic intellectual." George has advised the bishops to concentrate their authority on "the moral social" issues, such as abortion and same-sex marriage, and to curtail their lobbying for specific economic policies, such as the minimum wage and progressive tax rates. While the bishops have continued to lobby Congress on specific legislation, they have indeed invested a great deal of their moral capital opposing policies that threaten human life and the institution of marriage.

In his ministerial style as well as his interviews and writings, Pope Francis presents a much more integrated and joyful account of Christian discipleship in the contemporary world. Since becoming the Bishop of Rome on March 13, 2013, Francis has created an appealing public image of an authentic human being comfortably at peace with himself; a smiling pope energized by his heavy responsibilities; a dedicated pastor delighting in his interaction with children; and a respected spiritual leader joyfully proclaiming the persuasive power of divine love. In his significantly titled Apostolic Exhortation, *The Joy of the Gospel*, the Pope encourages the Christian faithful "to embark on a new chapter of evangelization" marked by "the joy of the gospel." A Christian dedicated to spreading the gospel message "must never look like someone who has just come back from a funeral!" (n. 10). There are, unfortunately, "Christians whose lives seem like Lent without Easter." Francis makes his own the famous warning of Pope John XXIII at the beginning of the Second Vatican Council against "the prophets of doom," who see in this modern age "nothing but prevarication and ruin" (n. 84). He also warns against "the disillusioned pessimists," who have lost trust in God and stifle the bold proclamation of the gospel (n. 85).

The joyful character of Christian discipleship flows from Christ himself, the ultimate source of our joy. As Francis states: "Our Christian joy drinks of the wellspring of his brimming heart" (n. 5). Jesus, who himself rejoiced in the Holy Spirit (Luke 10:21), promised to turn our sorrow into joy (John 16:20). The joy Christ gives us is a "missionary joy" that overcomes fear of the world and moves us "to go forth from our comfort zone" to reach those on the periphery in need of "the light of the Gospel" (n. 20).

Pope Francis not only provides a more positive and joyful outlook on Christian discipleship, he also challenges the assumption of the culture warriors that the essential mark of faithful Christians is vigorous opposition to abortion and gay marriage. *The Joy of the Gospel* develops this theme in the context of "pastoral ministry in a missionary style" (n. 34–39). In "today's world of instant communication," an overemphasis on moral issues presented out of context distorts "the heart of Christ's message" and deprives the proclamation of the Gospel of "what is most beautiful, most grand, most appealing and at the same time most necessary," the "basic core" that stresses "the beauty of the saving love of God made manifest in Jesus Christ who died and rose from the dead" (n. 34–36). "Before all else, the Gospel invites us to respond to the God of love who saves us, to see God in others, and to go forth from ourselves to seek the good of others" (n. 39). If this emphasis "does not radiate forcefully and effectively, the edifice of the Church's moral teaching risks becoming a house of cards, and this is our greatest risk" (n. 39). As these selected statements from his Apostolic Exhortation make clear, the pope is convinced that effective pastoral practice must present moral teachings in the context of the core gospel teachings on God's love. As such, it functions as an unmistakable challenge to the culture-war strategy.

In *The Joy of the Gospel*, Pope Francis challenges not only the culture-war strategy but also its fundamental sense of the way the church relates to the world. Instead of the stark vision of a persecuted church engaged in a clear-cut struggle against a culture of death, the pope reads the signs of the times and sees an ambivalent mix of sin and grace. He speaks of the delight and joy in proclaiming the living gospel in the contemporary world. Historically, wherever the good news of Christ has been preached and received, "the Holy Spirit enriches its culture with the transforming power of the Gospel" (n. 116). He finds it beautiful to see how many young people "are making common cause before the problems of our world and are taking up various forms of activism and volunteer work" (n. 106). Francis sees "the evils of our world" as "challenges which can help us grow" (n. 84). He takes a positive view of the new means of social communication, which, paradoxically, can produce "greater possibilities for encounter and solidarity for everyone" (n. 87). For him, contemporary culture, admittedly threatened by isolation, consumerism, and individualism, provides an opportunity for the church to offer healing, liberation, and fraternal communion for those with a "thirst for God."

Finally, Pope Francis offers an implied challenge to the sharp distinction between "tame Catholics," who do not fight vigorously enough against abortion and same-sex marriage, and "faithful Catholics," who are strong and consistent in opposition to those evils. In his Apostolic Exhortation, Francis takes up the issue of warfare among Christians (n. 98–101). He notes probable causes of this divisive mentality, including "a spirit of exclusivity" that creates an "inner circle" of believers who think of themselves as "different or special." In a world "torn apart by wars and violence, and wounded by a widespread individualism, which divides human beings," Francis implores "Christians in communities throughout the world to offer a radiant and attractive witness of fraternal communion." Recalling the heartfelt prayer of Jesus to the Father: "That they may all be one…in us, so that the world may believe" (John 17:21), the Pope urges Christians to "encourage and accompany one another," and "to rejoice in the gifts of each, which belong to all" (n. 100).

Francis deplores Christians who "desire to impose certain ideas at all costs, even to persecutions which appear as veritable witch hunts" (n. 100). The Pope concludes this section with an exhortation that Christian communities understand and follow the law of love, so that we do not allow ourselves to be robbed of the ideal of fraternal love!" (n. 101). Although Pope Francis speaks in general terms to the universal church, his vision of unity and harmony in the church can serve as a challenge to the culture warriors, who create divisions within the faith community by distinguishing tame and faithful Catholics, language that implicitly brands a large segment of the Catholic community as inferior. In summary, Pope Francis, by word and deed, provides a dialogic, collaborative approach to Christian discipleship that challenges the style, strategy, and substance of the culture-war viewpoint.

Encouraged by Francis, campus ministry maintains the dialogic approach to the academic world found in "The Quest for Wisdom." The church and the academy are in a common search for truth, goodness, and beauty. Both institutions can engage in a mutually beneficial dialogue that helps them realize their highest ideals. The university is an ambivalent mix of good and evil, as are all institutions including the church. With eyes of faith, campus ministers detect signs of grace as well as traces of sin. They can applaud, for example, the many contributions of the academy to the common good and its efforts to provide ethics courses in various fields such as medicine and business. Furthermore, campus ministry can also encourage universities to become more self-critical and to develop courses on university ethics that examine controversial issues such as the treatment of adjunct faculty and the role of revenue-producing sports. *Empowered by the Spirit* noted that the moral relativism on campus makes it "harder to mount an effective critique of institutional practices that violated the high ideals of higher education and fail to respect the dignity of human beings" (n. 62). This realistic assessment, however, does not absolve the church from joining in a new effort to promote honest and sustained reflection on university ethics. At the same time, the church must be open to criticism generated by the academic community: for example, the charge that belief is dehumanizing could spur efforts to develop a more vibrant Christian humanism.

As campus ministry engages the university in mutually critical dialogue, it does well to avoid the harsh divisive language of the culture warriors and to follow the example of Pope Francis, who prefers the more effective approach of honest encounter.

II

EMPOWERED
BY THE
SPIRIT

3

A THEOLOGICAL COMMENTARY

Following the rejection of "The Quest for Wisdom" by the bishops in June 1985, the editorial committee immediately began working on a revised document that concentrated less on the ministry to higher education and more on the internal life of the church on campus. During the summer of 1985, a new draft was written, criticized by the editorial committee, reviewed by an oversight committee and rewritten. This draft, amended slightly by the bishops in their Washington meeting, was officially issued on November 15, 1985, by the National Conference of Catholic Bishops with the title *Empowered by the Spirit: Campus Ministry Faces the Future*.

After discussing the history of campus ministry, its relationship with higher education, and its mission, the fifty-two-page pastoral presents six aspects or ministerial functions of campus ministry: Forming the Faith Community; Appropriating the Faith; Forming the Christian Conscience; Educating for Justice; Facilitating Personal Development; and Developing Leaders for the Future. Remarkably, these six functions have structured the training of campus ministers as well as the actual practice of campus ministry for over thirty years. The Catholic Campus Ministry Association, for example, still structures its annual convention around them. The campus ministers of Pennsylvania honored *Empowered by the Spirit* on its thirtieth anniversary at their November 2015 convention, which included my keynote address on the ongoing significance of the pastoral and workshops on its six aspects. Campus ministers with diverse theologies and serving at both secular and Catholic institutions have been able to use these ministerial functions to name and organize the services they offer. Using the term in a broad sense, we could speak of six "ministerial practices," that are fundamental to the work of the church on campus. The practices are inclusive: for example, not all campus ministry programs are able to provide eucharistic liturgies for their students, but all can try to create communal experiences for them, such as prayer groups or social action organizations. Campus ministers can use the functions as a basis for evaluating their programming: for instance, what are we doing to help form community among undergraduates, grad students, faculty, ourselves, and within the academic world? This grid can help identify strengths (e.g., a great retreat program) and weaknesses (e.g., not enough attention to social justice). A ministry team might find they are doing well in helping students learn leadership skills as officers in the Catholic Student Association but do nothing to help Catholic faculty and staff become better witnesses to their faith on campus.

The following commentary on *Empowered by the Spirit* summarizes the main points in the pastoral, and suggests ways of deepening and expanding some of its fundamental points.

A THEOLOGICAL COMMENTARY

Pastoral letters function best as catalysts for further reflection and as guides for practical action. They are the product of a lengthy process. By publication, they are, in some respects, already out of date. They are compromise documents that incorporate diverse interests and mediate divergent viewpoints. The theology employed in the text and its arguments tends to be conservative. Pastoral letters do not read like an exciting creative article by a theologian with a distinctive voice. They are documents that become acceptable to the entire body of bishops. The dominant concern of the hierarchy is not to break new ground theologically but to proclaim the traditional gospel and to provide unifying leadership for the church.

This analysis certainly applies to *Empowered by the Spirit: Campus Ministry Faces the Future*. As the writer for the editorial committee that produced the final draft, I was well acquainted with the compromises and accommodations necessary to gain the support of various segments of the bishops' conference. From the beginning of the drafting process, it was clear that the theology employed needed to be drawn selectively from official church teaching. A document acceptable to the bishops' conference simply had to reflect the theology found in the documents of the Second Vatican Council rather than the latest theological developments.

Working within this limited framework, the drafting committee did an excellent job of setting an acceptable direction for the final draft. They found ways to reincorporate essential elements of the rejected draft into the definitive version. For them it was important to convey some understanding of the innovative ministries being carried out on campuses. They were always mindful of creating a sense of the immense challenge and promise facing campus ministry today. They wanted the document to be as contemporary as possible in theological orientation. The practical wisdom and responsiveness to political realities demonstrated by my colleagues on the committee helped to produce a pastoral letter that, if not ideal, is still a workable springboard for further reflection and a handy guide for pastoral practice.

With this background, let's now consider some theological reflections on the text of the pastoral letter. We will begin with specific situations and experiences of the church on campus to indicate the essence of the pastoral's theological response and to suggest some areas for further development. The scope of this commentary will focus on the experience of traditional undergraduate students and will provide general observations and random comments on the theological significance of these experiences. Hopefully, by this approach, the whole church will benefit from a continuing examination of the life of faith communities on campus.

HISTORY AND CURRENT OPPORTUNITIES (4–12)

In the early phases of the Newman Movement, the hierarchy did not commit itself wholeheartedly to serving the needs and tapping the potential of students at public campuses.[1] Thus, students and their chaplains were forced to reflect and often did an admirable job of establishing Catholic communities on these campuses. However, they suffered from lack of support from the church and often fell into defensive postures in relationship to the university and other religious groups. In the pastoral letter, the bishops properly affirm and encourage the work of these students and their chaplains. For example, they provide a great deal of support for the church on campus when they state: "Campus ministry is an integral part of the church's mission to the world and must be seen in that light" (*Empowered*, n. 6). They endorse the improving relations between the church and university, and express their hopes for continued progress. Finally, the bishops encourage ecumenical and interfaith cooperation on individual campuses and affirm the diversity of styles and approaches that have been developed by Catholic campus ministry.

Developments in contemporary theology can help us ground and guide these distinctive experiences of the church on campus that the bishops have generally affirmed. Many trends help us appreciate the importance of the local faith community as the experiential base for Christian life. The approach to Christology developed by Edward Schillebeeckx insists that commitment to Christ must be founded not only on an interpreted understanding of the Gospels, but also on current experiences of the risen Christ available in local congregations.[2] Karl Rahner gives us an ecclesiology that centers on the local church and emphasizes the need for creative innovation so that the faith community can be a genuine sign of the kingdom and a catalyst for spiritual growth.[3] Leonardo Boff in *Church: Charism and Power* insists on the need for greater autonomy for the local church while maintaining its essential relationship with the universal church. Through his descriptions of base communities and their power to unleash the charisms of all the members, he suggests valuable ways to revitalize our faith communities on campus. Such contemporary theology reminds us that diverse experiences of the church on campus are not strange aberrations to be tolerated for strategic reasons. These experiences are legitimate expressions of Christian ecclesial life that deserve to be celebrated because they enrich the one church of Jesus Christ. The bond between the universal church and its local manifestations is essential and is rooted in the power of the Spirit who produces not uniformity but unity in diversity.

The current trends in ecumenical relationships on campus also deserve serious attention. The progress made since the Council is certainly a response to the prayer of the Good Shepherd that all his followers be united. Campuses have provided an ideal setting for overcoming prejudices, improving dialogue, and working together for the common good. At the same time, reflections on the kingdom ideal of living in mutual harmony highlight certain problem areas. For example, there have been several situations in which previously established institutional relationships among members of the mainline churches have broken down. Furthermore, campus ministers now spend a good deal of their time responding to the aggressive proselytizing efforts of exclusive fundamentalist groups. These groups that claim definitive scriptural answers to life's problems and employ the "love bombing" techniques of intensive personal attention continue to attract serious-minded Catholic students who are struggling with feelings of alienation and insecurity. The ideal of Christian unity demands that we keep searching for ways to dialogue with these aggressive groups and to find ways to work together in a more cooperative way.

Apart from the religious exclusivists, most collegians are ecumenically oriented. They are blissfully unaware of past confessional disputes and find the continuing divisions to be unintelligible and anachronistic. Many Catholic students are post-confessional Christians in that they function as though the various denominations were actually part of one Christian church. This does not mean that they are flocking to common worship services or participating widely in ecumenical activities. It does mean that they have tolerant attitudes, easily accept intercommunion, object to rigid church disciplines such as the mixed-marriage vows, and see no reason why we should not unite in one Christian family. It is as though they have ingested the spirit of Jesus' priestly prayer for unity, though in an uncritical way. In them we see embodied the sophisticated conclusions of important theologians such as Karl Rahner, who insists that all the outstanding theological disputes are solved in principle and that there is no reason why we cannot achieve unity among the main Christian denominations in the near future.[4] The whole church could profit by taking seriously the intuitive ecumenical spirit demonstrated by many Catholic students. At the same time, the students can benefit from the voice of experience that recognizes the danger of a mindless relativism. The balanced approach of the great ecumenist Yves Conger is an excellent guide in the search for a healthy ecumenism that is both faithful to our Catholic tradition and also open to cautious responses to the prompting of the Spirit.[5] This approach of making serious critical assessments of trends on campus in the light of the living Christian tradition could be extended to other current developments, such as volunteerism, an interest in lay ministry, the development of new attitudes toward human sexuality, and student involvement in the academic world. While campus life generally mirrors the entire society, it is also true that specific trends can be identified that show promise for challenging and enriching the whole church.[6]

CAMPUS MINISTRY AND THE RELATIONSHIP BETWEEN THE CHURCH AND HIGHER EDUCATION (13–21)

In the past, the church exercised a powerful influence on higher education. Today in the United States, the academic community is engaged in a lively debate and has initiated crucial reforms without any appreciable input from the Catholic Church. The only news we create in academic circles centers on the question of interference in academic freedom. The first draft of the pastoral letter, "The Quest for Wisdom," attracted a good deal of interest from leaders in the academic community. This is not surprising, since the editorial committee had close to three hundred responses from presidents and elected faculty leaders representing institutions of higher education from all fifty states who, in general, expressed great interest in the church's views on higher education. The published version of the pastoral letter, *Empowered by the Spirit*, has not made any direct impact on the public debate on higher education. It has received almost no publicity in the secular press. For instance, the "Chronicle of Higher Education" has never mentioned it. Interestingly, the pastoral does not directly address the problems of higher education and its scattered insights into these concerns are framed in ecclesial terms and placed in a ministerial context. It is crucial to keep this in mind; otherwise the approach of the pastoral letter could be used as a justification for campus ministry withdrawing to the periphery of campus life. Since the bishops decided not to enter the debate on higher education through this pastoral letter, the church on campus may be tempted to adopt the same posture and thus fail to play a role in local reforms. Without an official entrée, campus ministers may find it difficult to make their voices heard when decisions that affect the quality of life in the academic community are made. A pastoral letter that places so much emphasis on faith communities and employs a good deal of ecclesial language could be read as a warrant for settling into a Catholic enclave on the edge of the academic world.

Empowered by the Spirit offers its own response to this danger. It insists on the mutual benefit of a renewed dialogue between the church and higher education and suggests that the church possesses a wisdom tradition that could benefit the reform of education today.

A Theological Commentary

Throughout the letter there are repeated calls for active involvement by all segments of the church on campus in the life of the academic community. Catholic administrators, faculty members, and students have a responsibility to help their institutions realize their own potential for good and should be supported in this effort by the faith community. The letter, therefore, seeks to improve the quality of higher education not by contributing to the national debate but by encouraging responsible initiatives at the local level.

On my campus, for example, I gathered the president and all five vice presidents to discuss the first draft of the pastoral. They were very willing to participate and appreciated the church's distinctive insights. They are not interested in discussing *Empowered by the Spirit*. Now I meet regularly with the president of our student government, who sits on many university committees. I have given him copies of both drafts and have discussed their insights and suggestions with him. My hope is that, in this and other indirect ways, elements of our Christian wisdom tradition can be filtered into the general effort to improve the quality of academic life on our campus. The challenge of the pastoral is for campus ministers around the country to find their own ways of bringing our Catholic heritage to bear on the life of the academic community.

This challenge can be understood as part of the general theological question of the relationship between the church and the world. The Second Vatican Council, especially in its pastoral constitution, called for greater involvement in the contemporary world, which generally celebrates modern enlightenment values. This positive approach to the world is grounded in the theology of grace. The great God wills the salvation of all people (cf. 1 Tim 2:4) and to this end has entered a process of self-communication to the whole of creation and to all human beings. Following the lead of a long tradition recently retrieved by Karl Rahner, we can call this divine self-giving "uncreated grace." This self-communication as offered produces a universal revelation or inner word, which echoes in the call of conscience and creates an existential light illuminating the intellect. When this call is heeded and the heart is receptive, we are transformed, or divinized, as the Greek Fathers expressed it. This justifying grace brings us into a new relationship with the Father, helps us to put on the mind of Christ, and makes us responsive to the promptings of the Spirit. From this perspective, grace, though free, is not rare. We live and move and have our being in one graced world. God's grace permeates the entire cosmos and

57

all dimensions and aspects of human existence. Only sin, personal and social, can screen out the power of God's self-giving. Thus, all things are potentially revelatory. Persons, communities, religions, and institutions can all be catalysts for a deeper understanding and appreciation of the divine-human relationship. At the same time, no created reality can exhaust or control the Gracious Mystery that has communicated itself to us. Of course, for Christians, God's self-giving and human receptivity have met definitively, irrevocably, and with complete fullness in Jesus of Nazareth. He is the final prophet and the absolute savior. The scriptures that officially witness to his life, death, and resurrection provide us with criteria for making judgments about the validity of insights and inspirations that arise in the culture and in social institutions. The uniqueness of Christ and the New Testament is inclusive rather than exclusive. Christianity illumines rather than vitiates the truth, goodness, and beauty that emerge in our one, graced world.

This sketch of a Rahnerian-inspired theology of grace is the basis of the call for a renewed dialogue between church and higher education.[7] We approach the university as an institution that is a mixture of grace and sin, just as we experience the church as saved but sinful. Without claiming all the answers and willing to learn from each other, we have the twin tasks of searching for a truth that always remains inexhaustible and of working to improve society, which always remains imperfect.

Since the Council, some theologians have challenged an uncritical acceptance of the modern world, which they see reflected in its *Pastoral Constitution on the Church in the Modern World (Gaudium et spes)*.[8] Theologians, influenced by liberation themes, are much attuned to the contradictions in society, the oppressive structures, and the silenced voices of those on the margins. From this perspective, the modern values of rational discourse and scientific progress that are celebrated in the university must be criticized. We must ask in what ways the university fosters naïve optimism, rationalism, materialism, scientism, and sexism. The God of the Exodus opposes all idols, including modern efforts to invest finite realities with absolute value. Jesus Christ the liberator challenges all the narrow notions of humanity that exclude individuals and force groups to the margins. If the church on campus is inspired by these biblical themes, it will function as a countercultural community and as an advocate for the dispossessed. It will also become more self-critical, searching out the ideological elements in its own self-understanding and mode of operating.

The pastoral letter locates campus ministry "where commitment to Christ and care for the academic world meet in purposeful activity to serve and realize the kingdom of God" (*Empowered*, n. 21). In the light of the liberationists' critique of liberal theology, this purposeful activity grounded in commitment to Christ must have a strong critical element if it is to help establish the kingdom of justice.

THOSE WHO SERVE ON CAMPUS (22–32)

There are several important developments among the people who constitute the church on campus. More laypeople and increasing numbers of women are serving as campus ministers and exercising leadership in the faith community. In some situations, they perform, without benefit of ordained clergy, the pastoral functions of gathering, coordinating, educating, and comforting, as well as leading prayer and encouraging action on behalf of justice. Peer ministry is also expanding as campus ministers learn the value of training students to share their faith and to serve other students in a variety of ways. Some faith communities place the peer ministry approach at the very center of their programs. Finally, team ministry has become the dominant style for the campus ministers. There are, indeed, competing theories on how teams should function and a certain amount of conflict is inevitable as individuals learn to work collaboratively. However, there is a sense that the team approaches developed on campuses not only increase ministerial effectiveness, but serve as models of ministry and community for the rest of the church.

In the pastoral letter, the bishops affirm essential elements in these various developments. They maintain that people are more important than programs, that all the members of the church on campus are co-responsible for its well-being, and that the church is enriched by a more diverse representation of people involved in campus ministry. In addition, they recognize that service to the academic community is a vital exercise of baptismal responsibilities and that team ministry is an exemplary development. However, the experience of campus ministers is too rich and too diverse to be contained in the theological models employed by the letter. For example, some women ministers who function as the real leaders of the faith community are frustrated and angry because they must bring in an ordained priest to preside at the Eucharist. They find support in theologians who dissent from the official position on women's ordination,[9] and detect a practical solution in Karl Rahner's suggestion that faith communities discern their genuine leaders, who are then ordained by the bishop to lead the community and preside at the Eucharist.[10] These examples show that an examination of the full range of the experience of Catholics on campus puts pressure on our current theological models and suggests the need for more creative theological reflection.

FORMING THE FAITH COMMUNITY (34–44)

Campus ministers place great emphasis on forming faith communities and often achieve impressive results. Visitors to residential campuses are frequently impressed by the large numbers of students who gather for Mass and participate enthusiastically. On commuter campuses, creative ministers have found ways to form less visible but still vibrant communities around shared prayer, Bible study, and service projects. We are producing large numbers of collegians who have experienced warm, welcoming, active, participative Christian communities on campus. They have come to expect liturgies that are flexible and speak to their real concerns. Retreats have provided them with opportunities to discuss their faith as well as their personal struggles.

Forming faith communities must be a high priority for campus ministry because, by its very nature, Christianity is ecclesial. The communal character of salvation is already clear in the Hebrew Scriptures. The bishops of the Second Vatican Council stated the point clearly: "It has pleased God, however, to make human beings holy and save them, not merely as individuals without any mutual bonds, but by making them into a single people, a people which acknowledges Him in truth and serves Him in holiness."[11] While contemporary theology insists that Jesus did not personally set up an ecclesial organization, it also insists on the community-building significance of much of his teaching activity.[12] He chose the Twelve, which symbolically represented the new people of God. His teaching broke down barriers and gathered people into the community of love. Through his miracles, he not only cured the sick but enabled them to overcome their ostracized status and to return to participation in the life of the community. The death and resurrection of Jesus brought a new sense of solidarity. Guided by the Spirit, the church continues to function as the visible sign of the unity of the whole human family and as an instrument of reconciliation for all.

We are familiar with many images of the church, such as institution, herald, community, servant, and sacrament.[13] However, the experience of the church on campus suggests two other models: sacrament of the Spirit and community of ministers.

The notion of the church as sacrament of the Spirit, which has been developed by Leonardo Boff[14] and others, fits in well with the empowerment theme of the pastoral letter. This model encourages the use of feminine imagery and suggests fluid boundaries. It also highlights the charisms each member receives to make the community into a credible sign of the kingdom. The section of the pastoral that provides the theological base for the formation of Christian communities has a striking pneumatological character (*Empowered*, n. 36). Thus, the Spirit, which animates all human beings, leads Jesus during his earthly life and is communicated in a unique way to his followers through the paschal mystery. The same Spirit brings growth and integrity to the church by calling it to be mindful of the priestly prayer of Jesus for unity and by guiding it to be a credible sign of the oneness of the whole human family. Empowered by the Spirit, all the baptized are responsible for forming the church into a genuine community of worship and service. This emphasis in the pastoral already indicates some of the advantages of imaging the church as sacrament of the Spirit.

The other model suggested by the campus experiences is the church as a community of ministers. This is more explicitly active than the model of the community of disciples proposed by Avery Dulles to capture essential elements of the postconciliar Catholic experience.[15] Every member possesses gifts and talents that can be used for building up the kingdom in the world. All are co-responsible for the well-being of the faith community. The model also suggests that the members are called to minister to one another and that there is a mutuality of giving and receiving between leaders and other members of the church. The practice of peer ministry and team ministry, which characterizes the church on campus, fits well into this model. There is a danger that the less active members might feel excluded from the community that tries to live out this conception of the church. A broad notion of ministry and gentle invitations to greater involvement can help overcome this problem. Regardless, we must take the distinctive experience of the campus church seriously and, when we do, new models will emerge.

APPROPRIATING THE FAITH (45–58)

Most Catholic collegians are handicapped by an inadequate understanding of their faith. Some are angry and frustrated by the poor religious education they have received. Few seem prepared to do anything constructive about this. The religious illiteracy rampant in society simply exacerbates the problem. Catholic students become aware of the difficulty when their faith is challenged or latent doubts emerge. This may occur through dealing with challenging course material, coming face to face with suffering, meeting people with diverse worldviews, or encountering aggressive fundamentalists on campus.

In general, campus ministers have not been very successful in dealing with this problem of religious illiteracy. Over time, some effective programs have established a tradition of theological education; others have found ways to give academic credit for religion courses taught at their own centers or have succeeded in improving the religious studies offerings on campus.

The pastoral letter properly insists on the importance of achieving an adult appropriation of the faith, based on both the nature of Christianity and the purpose of education. It speaks well about the role of theology in keeping alive the great questions and suggests some helpful strategies for overcoming religious illiteracy. However, among collegians the problem is that theology itself has a bad reputation. They think of it as too abstract and out of touch with their experience. Unfortunately, some of their encounters with classic works and even well-known contemporary theologians have reinforced their negative feelings. We get some sense of the problem by recalling that the great European theologian, Edward Schillebeeckx, claimed he wrote his long, erudite book, *Jesus,* to bridge the gap between academic theology and the ordinary person. The key to teaching theology to today's collegians is to ground the whole enterprise totally and unambiguously in their experience. This requires a methodological change and an understanding of the collegiate experience that most of our leading theologians have not yet accomplished despite their common insistence on experience as a legitimate source for theological reflection. Perhaps we need to learn a lesson from the Christian base communities about which the liberation theologians write. Following their example, we could gather collegians for theological reflection on some of their common experiences, ranging from rock concerts and campus lectures to liturgical prayer and service projects. This would, of course, not provide a systematic overview of theology, but would at least have the advantage of being rooted in their experience. A problem, here, is finding leaders who know the Christian tradition and are comfortable in unstructured settings. In the long run, the insistence of collegians on a rigorously experiential theology will prove beneficial to all of us.

FORMING THE CHRISTIAN CONSCIENCE (50–69)

Catholic collegians, who are moving through various stages of moral development, must cope with a confusing combination of moral relativism and peer pressure to conform. During my years of campus ministry, I have been greatly impressed with individual students who rise above the crowd and maintain their gospel values in the face of immense pressures. At the same time, there are many others who need help just to begin the process of thinking critically about moral questions, as a first step toward greater moral maturity.

Through the pastoral letter, the bishops present a traditional balanced view of conscience, which includes both the objective call from God and the need for an intelligent, free response. They present a model of the mature Christian who has put on the mind of Christ and is thus able to live out a responsible freedom and a generous love.

On a personal level, students fight not only moral relativism, but also guilt and cynicism. They are often disappointed with their failures to live up to their own ideals. When this happens, it is easy to fall into either neurotic guilt or cynical pessimism. The temptation is to say either "I am no good" or "why bother trying." This is the kind of situation that makes the work of moral theologians such as Bernard Haring and Charles Curran so valuable.[16] They remind us that the radical ethical teaching of Jesus, represented in the New Testament, functions as a moral ideal, rather than as an absolute law that admits of no exceptions. The Gospel presents us with a thrust toward perfection that can never be totally attained. Students need to hear both a consistent call to become their better selves as well as a merciful word that recognizes the harsh realities of life and the weaknesses of human nature. Christian ideals are always worthy of our best efforts, but always remain beyond our grasp. This healthy tension is precisely the way around both the paralyzing guilt and deadening cynicism. We should also build on the solid base of the pastoral letter by putting more emphasis on the role of imagination, story, and virtue in conscience formation.[17] Morality is firstly a matter of who we are, rather than what we do. We are rediscovering the scholastic axiom that action follows being. Our imagination must be structured by positive images of the good life. In scriptural terms, we are called to put on the mind of Christ. Our life story should be in tune with the gospel. We are called to cultivate virtue so we can do good spontaneously and with pleasure. Thus, conscience formation is broader than applying scriptural quotes from church teachings. We need living examples, inspiring stories, and positive images. Christ must become real for us in the scriptures and in individuals who manifest his Spirit.

EDUCATING FOR JUSTICE (70–82)

Regarding social justice, campus life largely reflects the apathy of the culture. However, within this situation, we also find small groups of committed Christian students who buck the prevailing trends and continue the struggle for peace and justice. They make mistakes and learn as they go. Their knowledge of Catholic social teaching is usually limited but their passion for justice is expansive indeed. Some burn out and others get co-opted into the system, but the ones who maintain their commitments are living reminders of the social dimension of the gospel and the liberating power of the Spirit.

The pastoral letter notes and encourages this activity on behalf of justice and insists that the works of justice are not optional nor the task of only a few, but the responsibility of all. The bishops highlight the biblical model of Jesus Christ the liberator and summarize the major themes found in modern Catholic social thought. They reject the haven of mere theorizing as well as the utopian world of naïve idealism. Instead, they insist on concrete practical activity that flows from an informed assessment of the real situation.

To intensify the already strong claims of the pastoral letter, we turn to the liberation theologies developed by spokespersons for the oppressed[18] as well as to the various political theologies that take societal systems seriously.[19] These theologians invite us to reread the scriptures from the viewpoint of the poor and the oppressed. Social sin is emphasized, especially its power to imprison groups on the margins and to create false consciousness in all segments of the society. They raise up the dangerous memory of Jesus with his power to cut through our complacency and self-righteousness. Liberation theology has also developed a spirituality based on the prophetic experience of solidarity with the poor that could provide inspiration and enlightenment for the committed Christian activist on campus.

Nevertheless, it would be a mistake to think that we could simply borrow a theology from other contexts that will illumine and guide our efforts on behalf of social justice here in the United States. We need a theology that grows out of our distinctive experience. In this regard, we could profit from a rereading of Reinhold Niebuhr, who demonstrated the transforming power of the gospel by bringing it into a critical contact with the political and economic questions of his time and place.[20] We will also find practical guidance from Martin Luther King, who was a far better theologian than commonly assumed and who developed a liberation theology rooted in the experience of powerlessness in the United States. A reading of the various liberation theologies suggests that we should gather small groups of social activists, including students, faculty members, and chaplains, to organize, carry out, and reflect on specific justice and peace projects. Faculty members would supply expertise on the issue; students would provide the point of contact with the realities of campus life; and the chaplains would lead subsequent prayerful reflections on the deeper meaning of the shared experience. Out of this kind of reflection on praxis, multiplied on campuses around the country, we could begin to work out an indigenous liberation theology.

FACILITATING PERSONAL DEVELOPMENT (83–92)

While colleges and universities offer marvelous opportunities for personal development, many students miss these opportunities by concentrating exclusively on getting a degree in order to secure a lucrative job. At the same time, an informal process of personal growth inevitably goes on during the collegiate years, even if it has not been reflected upon. Students are intensely interested in learning to cope with their own problems and to relate better with others. There is an ideal of the self-actualized person that pervades the academic community. It is primarily individualistic and concentrates either on gaining technical competency or achieving self-fulfillment. Members of the faith community share in this ideal and the independent search it often fosters.

The strategy of the pastoral is to affirm the ideal for full personal development while placing it in a Christian context. Thus "Christians must proclaim an ideal of self-fulfillment that is solidly rooted in the sacredness of person, is placed in the service of the common good, and stays open to the God who is the source of all growth" (87). The bishops wisely refused to cede this whole area of personal development to the humanists. They therefore present the model of Christian humanists, who have integrated the legitimate meaning and values of the culture within a comprehensive and organic framework built on faith in Jesus Christ. The believing humanists understand that personal development is a lifelong process in which sin contends with a more powerful grace. The bishops insist that the ideal of Christian humanism must be proclaimed as a more attractive alternative to the individualistic self-fulfillment model.

This notion of Christian humanism is worth developing in greater detail. It could guide a great deal of pastoral work that connects with students precisely at the point of their intense desire for personal growth. The model of Christian humanism can collect the wisdom of those who have achieved an integrated synthesis in the past and place this wisdom in a contemporary framework. We can retrieve the thoughts of Augustine, Aquinas, and Newman by placing their insights into a context that is more open to process and the continual search for the truly human. Within this framework, I envision spiritual direction that promotes holistic growth, seminars on personal development that root the process in community life, courses on self-actualization that draw on the Christian tradition and thematic liturgies that celebrate personal development as a call and gift from God.

DEVELOPING LEADERS FOR THE FUTURE (93–101)

The common statement that today's collegians are tomorrow's leaders deserves attention. In the future, most of the students will exercise some form of leadership in their families and in their careers. Some of them will become more prominent leaders and will be able to exert considerable influence. The collegiate years provide rich opportunities to explore possibilities and to prepare for future involvement in the world. Today's students tend to think of their future roles in terms of the privatism and individualism dominant in the culture. Against this general trend is the dedication of individual students who desire to serve the common good, to be involved in public service, and to contribute to the life of the church.

The pastoral letter places leadership in a Christian perspective. It highlights the New Testament ideal of leadership as loving service to the community as well as the call of the Second Vatican Council for proper preparation to develop the gifts of the Spirit for the good of others. It employs a broad notion of vocation based on baptism, which gives Christians living in various states of life the task of bringing gospel values to bear on temporal affairs.

The letter also calls on campus ministers to promote vocations to the priesthood but without examining the root causes of the current problem. The difficulty is not lack of dedication and interest. Campus ministers know this well from their involvement with a considerable number of collegians who defy peer pressure and cultural trends by living out a genuine and inspiring commitment to Christ. The real problems are mandatory celibacy and the exclusion of women that reduces the pool of potential recruits. This, in turn, makes it harder for parents and priests today to recommend the priesthood enthusiastically. Historical studies by theologians have relativized the mandatory celibacy law by pointing out that it became the explicit law for the Western church only at the Second Lateran Council in 1139, and that it was based on questionable attitudes toward human sexuality.[21] Today, there are committed collegians who have a more positive attitude toward sexuality and find it hard to see any connection between priestly service and giving up marriage. The experience and outlook of these young people should be taken seriously in theological reflection on vocations to the priesthood.

In general, the theology of baptism suggested by the pastoral letter can be a fruitful way of approaching the leadership question. Recent studies make us more aware of the way baptism calls all Christians to use the gifts of the Spirit for the common good. Baptism prepares us for responsible service in any state of life. As Rahner suggests, holy orders can be seen as a specification of the consecration already given by baptism.[22] This line of thought can help to promote Christian leadership among all members of the faith community and to demonstrate the possibilities for witnessing to the gospel in all circumstances of life.

EPILOGUE (103–5)

As the pastoral letter proclaims, campus ministry today is indeed at the beginning of a new era. The bishops have done us a great service and played their proper role by articulating a vision of that future. It is common in theology today to speak about "orthopraxis," which suggests that Christians are called not only to proclaim the gospel teaching in a faithful manner, but to put kingdom ideals into actual practice. To live in this way requires a hopeful realism, which faces the limitation and harshness of human existence but maintains trust that God in his tender mercy will never abandon us. The real test of the pastoral letter is whether it motivates all segments of the church to proclaim and practice the message of Christ in creative ways that take seriously the continually developing pastoral situation on campuses. Finally, theological reflection should cultivate prayerful attitudes. Thus, empowered by the Spirit, we consciously place ourselves in the hands of the Gracious Mystery, who gives deeper meaning to all our efforts to spread the kingdom in the academic world.

DIALOGUE WITH FRANCIS

In this section, we engage Francis on three of the pastoral functions: facilitating personal development; forming the Christian conscience; and preparing leaders. The other three aspects will be treated later in the book.

FACILITATING PERSONAL DEVELOPMENT

As campus ministry presents an attractive Christian humanism as a guide for those on campus seeking self-fulfillment, Pope Francis puts a human face on that abstract ideal. For Christians, Jesus Christ is the supreme model of fulfilled human existence, the most fully actualized person, the best respondent to the call of the Father. Traditionally, we honor exceptional individuals who manifest Christ-like virtues as saints and look to them for guidance in our own quest for holiness. For many people, Pope Francis already plays this role. He represents the intrinsic power of gospel ideals. He not only speaks compellingly about the joy of the gospel, but radiates that joy in his daily activities. The media culture has made him into a celebrity but he seems to operate out of an inner core that is immune to the temptations that typically accompany celebrity status. He can interact with the famous and the powerful but is even more at home with the poor and marginalized. Ordinary people see him as an authentic person, one who not only talks the talk but walks the walk. His call to care for the poor rings true because of his own ministry to the marginalized in his native Argentina. His message about the value of a simpler lifestyle gains credibility because he lives in the Vatican guesthouse and eats in the cafeteria. Even prominent critics of the pope's position on global warming consider him to be a saint. One of his great virtues is humility. He does not lord it over others but sees himself as a servant leader. He addresses the poor and imprisoned as sisters and brothers. His self-identification as a sinner resonates with many people. His frequent requests for prayer seem to be an expression of a truly humble heart that recognizes total dependence on God and solidarity with other persons.

During his six-day visit to the United States, Francis demonstrated truly remarkable physical endurance for a 78-year-old man with one lung and an ailing leg. It seems he drew on a source of inner energy that Christians name the Holy Spirit, and was energized by his contact with the poor and powerless. In diverse situations, he seemed at ease, comfortable in his own skin, present to the moment, attentive to the people he encountered. He presided at liturgies with an unaffected reverence, addressed Congress with full confidence despite his accented English, and spoke in Spanish to a large crowd before Independence Hall in Philadelphia with an infectious spontaneous enthusiasm. Some of those fortunate individuals who encountered him personally described the moment as life-changing. People who waited hours just to get a glimpse of him said it was worthwhile. Millions watched him on television, drawn by some mysterious qualities that defy easy analysis in familiar terms. Perhaps we could say we were captivated by a man fully alive to the glory of God, a sinner who believes in the redemptive power of Christ, a leader who mediates the "surpassing power" of the Holy Spirit, a Christian humanist who makes the gospel message of love and mercy attractive, and a pope who revives the liberating spirit of the Second Vatican Council.

In Pope Francis, campus ministry has a rich and compelling resource for facilitating personal development. He points away from himself to Christ, the supreme example of self-fulfillment. He challenges narrow notions of self-actualization that are egocentric and disconnected from community interests. He exemplifies a Christian humanism that is engaged with the world, prefers dialogue to confrontation, and maintains a joyful, hopeful spirit despite the challenges of the postmodern world. By word and example, he reminds us that personal development is for the sake of serving others more diligently and promoting the common good more effectively.

Wise campus ministers look for ways to use Francis in their programming. He can serve as a model of virtue in homilies. Lectures and seminars can examine the theology that grounds his Christian humanism. Students can collect quotes from him that energize and guide their personal development. They can search the internet for favorite images of his visit to the United States and share them on social media. The wide public exposure of Pope Francis and his continuing popularity make him a compelling model for collegians seeking fulfillment.

For Francis, personal development is about becoming a saint. Holiness is not the prerogative of a select few; it is rather a gift God offers to all, with no exceptions, so that it constitutes the distinctive mark of all Christians. Members of the church on campus pursue authentic holiness by meeting their daily responsibilities: students by participating in campus life, attending class, and working hard on their assignments; faculty members by caring for their students, preparing class, and doing research; campus ministers by functioning as genuine servant leaders, being available to the community, and providing opportunities for prayer and service. Campus ministers inspired by Francis will promote authentic personal development by stressing the universal call to holiness directed to all its members.

FORMING THE CHRISTIAN CONSCIENCE

For Pope Francis, Jesus himself is the supreme model for following conscience. He was not a "remote-controlled" automaton who automatically knew what was right and wrong in every situation. Like us, he prayed to discern God's will and struggled to be faithful to the voice of his Father heard deep in the inner sanctuary of his conscience. Faithful to God's will, he sought every moment of his life to give glory to the Father. He did this by living out the law of love he proclaimed: demonstrating a "closeness" to those he encountered; looking into their eyes with concern; being accessible to those in need; eating and drinking with sinners without worrying about being thought of as a "glutton and drunkard" himself; allowing a sinful woman to anoint his feet; and welcoming Nicodemus who came to him at night. As Francis insists, "the sacrifice of Jesus on the cross is nothing else than 'the culmination of the way he lived his entire life'" (*The Joy of the Gospel*, n. 269).

Formed by the example of Christ, our task is "to enter fully into the fabric of society," listening to others and helping them in their material and spiritual needs. We are called to read the signs of the times and to collaborate in building a better world. We do all this not out of "a sense of obligation, nor as a burdensome duty" but because of "a personal decision" to follow Christ that "brings us joy and gives meaning to our lives" (*The Joy of the Gospel*, n. 269). This account of the Christian life makes it clear that following our conscience is not a matter of doing whatever interests or pleases us, but of listening to the voice of the Lord who helps us to discern the right path and to follow it faithfully.

Reflection on the formation of conscience cannot avoid considering the striking self-identification of Pope Francis: "I am a sinner." A properly formed Christian conscience recognizes both the amazing gift of God's unconditional love for us and the limited, incomplete, sinful character of our response. The harsh truth is that we sometimes disappoint ourselves by failing to live up to the noble ideals of the gospel. A comprehensive examination of conscience reveals both virtues and vices, the good and the bad, acts of love and selfishness, moments of courage and cowardice. Francis teaches us to thank God for progress made despite our sinfulness. For him Christian morality is not so much about "never falling down" but more about "always getting up" with God's merciful help.

DEVELOPING LEADERS FOR THE FUTURE

Campus ministry does well to examine the teaching and example of Pope Francis on leadership. Addressing his brother bishops and priests on various occasions, Francis has issued some stern warnings. He told newly appointed cardinals to avoid jealous rivalry and to reject intrigue, gossip, cliques, and favoritism typical of kingly courts. He has often reminded priests to live simple, humble, authentic, and holy lives so as to offer effective, professional service to their people. The church does not need bishops who are "apologists for their own agendas," but does need humble and faithful sowers of the truth." The pope has blasted bishops who are ambitious career climbers, who strut around in church finery like "peacocks," who have the "psychology of princes," and who commit "adultery" by seeking a more prestigious diocese. In his speech to some three hundred bishops in Washington, the pope encouraged them to be shepherds fortified by prayer and a "trusting union with Christ." They should avoid "harsh and divisive language" and promote "a culture of encounter," relying fearlessly on the method of dialogue out of fidelity to Christ and respect for the people they serve. Refreshed by Christ, bishops have the primary responsibility of solidifying and maintaining the unity of the church. The Year of Mercy, which began on December 8, 2015, was a "privileged moment" for "perfecting unity, reconciling differences, forgiving one another, and healing every rift." By taking on this leadership role, the bishops perform a great service to their country and provide a beacon of light for those "sailing through the dark clouds of life." Francis concluded his talk to the bishops with two admonitions: be close to your people and welcome immigrants who enrich the country and the church.

Campus ministry can also learn from the spiritual journey of Jorge Bergoglio as a Jesuit priest in Argentina. After spending thirteen years as a Jesuit novice, he was ordained a priest in 1969 at the age of 33, took his permanent vows a year later and a fourth vow of papal loyalty in 1973. Recognized for certain leadership skills, he was appointed the provincial superior of all the Jesuits in Argentina from 1973 to 1979, after which he served as the rector of the Jesuit seminary near Buenos Aires. During those years, Argentina was amid violent turmoil, including the so-called Dirty War that lasted from 1976 to 1983. The Jesuits were divided between progressives, who favored the newly developed liberation theology and grassroots efforts to help the poor, and conservatives, who were inclined to continue their traditional educational mission. According to Paul Vallely, writing in the August 2015 issue of the *Atlantic Monthly*, Bergoglio became an increasingly polarizing leader in the Jesuit community. The progressives saw him as an opponent of liberation theology and as an authoritarian who was not open to opposing views. Francis himself has admitted he was too young and immature to handle the leadership responsibilities thrust upon him at such an early age, which led him to make quick decisions without proper consultation. By 1990, he had become such a polarizing figure and lost so much support among the Argentine Jesuits that his superior in Rome sent him to Cordoba, a large city some four hundred miles from Buenos Aires where, according to Vallely, he was ostracized from his peers, carefully monitored, and forbidden to say public Masses in the Jesuit church. During his two years in Cordoba, "a time of great interior crisis," as Francis later called it, he heard many confessions, interacted with the poor, and spent a good deal of time in prayerful self-reflection. When he returned to Buenos Aires, as auxiliary bishop in 1992, his leadership style had changed dramatically; less authoritarian and more consultative. During his exile in Cordoba, Bergoglio developed the virtue of humility, which serves, according to Vallely, as "a tool" in his struggle against "the rigid, authoritarian and egotistical" tendencies in his own personality.

The Cordoba story is crucial to appreciating the leadership style of Pope Francis. He learned from his many mistakes as a young Jesuit superior. He now consciously tries to follow the example of Jesus, who came not to be served but to serve, as graphically illustrated at the Last Supper when he washed the feet of his disciples. He goes out of his way to listen to others and to learn from genuine dialogue with them. We could interpret his consistent practice of asking for prayers as one of his ways of cultivating a humility that accepts complete dependence on God. His frequent references to the teachings of national hierarchies exemplify his conviction that the Bishop of Rome is not the reigning expert on every issue. Francis has learned that consultation and dialogue produce better decisions and more effective results.

Campus ministers do well to ponder the spiritual journey of Jorge Bergoglio from an opinionated authoritarian to a genuine servant leader. It is possible to overcome pride and develop the virtue of humility. Leaders of the campus church can become better listeners and do a better job of spotting talent and coordinating charisms. They can delegate responsibilities more effectively if they trust the Spirit is at work in the whole community of faith. Asking for prayers can promote solidarity if it is an authentic faith-driven request. Francis directs us to Christ as the humble servant and suggests ways to represent him in our complex, pluralistic, postmodern world.

Pope Francis insists on the role of all baptized Christians in carrying out the message of the church (*The Joy of the Gospel*, 119–21). The Spirit guides the people of God, furnishing them with "an instinct of faith" that helps them grasp intuitively "divine realities" and serve as "agents of evangelization." Every Christian has a vocation to be a missionary, drawing on their experience of God's love manifested in Christ. We are all called "to communicate Jesus wherever we are," giving witness to the deep truth that he "gives meaning to our lives." Even our failures to live this vocation adequately serve as "a constant stimulus" not to stay "mired in mediocrity" but to continue walking the path of spiritual growth. As the pope insists, we are all "called to mature" in our evangelizing task. The church must provide "better training" so that we all see ourselves as "missionary disciples" prepared to give "clearer witness to the Gospel."

The church on campus has the important responsibility of providing the kind of training for missionary discipleship envisioned by Francis. Traditional-aged students are in a process of forming their identity and preparing for a career. Older students are often rethinking the purpose and direction of their lives. Campus ministry encourages collegians to recognize their vocation to Christian discipleship that can be carried out in any legitimate path they choose to follow. They are in college not just to get a degree that leads to a lucrative job but to prepare for a life of Christian witness.

Campus ministry in the United States provides a wide variety of programs that help prepare students for future leadership roles in the church and society, including marriage preparation programs, Christian service projects, active student organizations, liturgical training, small-group discussions for those interested in church ministry, and spiritual direction for those considering the priesthood and religious life. In the planning and execution of these efforts, campus ministers should be mindful of the advice from Francis: by virtue of baptism all Christians have a vocation to build up the Body of Christ and spread the reign of God in the world; all Christians have gifts and talents given to promote the common good; Christians do not need to be perfect in order to be effective leaders; failures in leadership can be a catalyst for spiritual growth; all discipleship has a missionary thrust; Christians can be active evangelizers in any career and in all situations; and, of central importance, Christ is the supreme model for doing God's will in the world. Learning from Francis is a wonderful way to improve the ministerial function of developing leaders for the future.

4

IMPLEMENTING THE PASTORAL LETTER

In 2000, the editor of *Crossroads*, the journal of the Catholic Campus Ministry Association, invited me to write an article on the fifteenth anniversary of the publication of *Empowered by the Spirit*. At the time, I was pastor of Corpus Christi University Parish serving the University of Toledo, a large state institution, and helping campus ministers improve their ministry at smaller universities and two-year commuter colleges in the Diocese of Toledo. Periodically, campus ministers in other parts of the country invited me to give talks on their campuses, which gave me a broader view of how *Empowered by the Spirit* was being implemented, as did my interactions with new campus ministers at some of the annual Frank J. Lewis summer institutes.

During this period, *Empowered by the Spirit* continued to guide the ministry of the church on campus. In 1996, for example, the Department of Education of the United States Catholic Conference published a 232-page resource manual entitled "The Gospel on Campus: A Handbook of Campus Ministry Programs and Resources" (second edition). Produced under the general editorship of Dr. Michael Galligan-Stierle, it included articles by more than thirty campus ministers, organized around the general outline of *Empowered by the Spirit* with its six main ministerial functions. My brief article suggested that it is helpful to explore various dimensions or typical characteristics that should inform all the ministerial functions. So, for example, campus ministry should have a spiritual dimension aimed at helping all the baptized become more attuned to the will of God; an interfaith dimension designed to promote dialogue among the various religious traditions on campus; and an evangelizing dimension promoting an outreach to inactive Catholics and unchurched seekers. A twenty-five-page section of the handbook was devoted to these dimensions of campus ministry, followed by a detailed treatment of the six ministerial functions. Significantly, the influence of the pastoral letter continued into the new millennium. In 2002, for example, the bishops' Committee on Education published "Empowering Campus Ministry: A Condensed Version of *Empowered by the Spirit*," a short, thirteen-page document intended to offer prayerful support, encouragement, and guidance to campus ministers. Two years later, the bishops published "Student Leaders Guide to Campus Ministry," which again followed and applied the structure and major points of *Empowered by the Spirit*.

EMPOWERED AT AGE FIFTEEN[1]

Despite the momentous changes in our culture, *Empowered by the Spirit* remains remarkably relevant. It still encourages broad creative approaches by locating campus ministry at that exciting and challenging intersection where "commitment to Christ and care for the academic world meet in purposeful activity to serve and realize the kingdom of God" (n. 21). It retains the general thrust of the initial draft document, "The Quest for Wisdom," calling for ongoing dialogue between the church and the university, based on the conviction that collaboration between these "two great institutions" is "indispensable to the health of society" (n. 13).

By grounding its discussion of those who serve on campus in a theology of baptism, the pastoral encourages all Catholic students, faculty, and staff members "to bring Christian witness to the academic world," while recognizing the crucial task of professional campus ministers to provide strong leadership for the faith community and to coordinate the diverse gifts of all its members (n. 23, 24). Since its publication, the six aspects of campus ministry delineated in the letter (Forming the Faith Community, Appropriating the Faith, Forming the Christian Conscience, Educating for Justice, Facilitating Personal Development, and Developing Leaders) have been consistently helpful in providing a grid for preparing, planning, organizing, and evaluating campus ministry programs and activities. This template works especially well when it is applied to our ministry to the academic community as well as within the faith community, and includes care for students, faculty, staff members, and ourselves as professional campus ministers. Finally, the bishops made a significant commitment, which is still in place, to provide well-educated, adequately-funded ministers who "can serve as on-campus sources of spiritual and intellectual assistance" (n. 103, 104).

Empowered by the Spirit has worked best as a catalyst for comprehensive and creative approaches to campus ministry. Across the country, we have done well in some areas: facilitating personal development through counseling, spiritual direction, and general encouragement; providing leadership opportunities through our student organizations; and forming community through good liturgies, prayer groups, common efforts to help the needy, and retreats that attract large numbers of students. We have done less well in overcoming religious illiteracy and helping those we serve to achieve a more mature understanding of their faith. Our attempts to educate for justice through advocacy programs for institutional change based on Catholic social teaching have not been as successful as the service projects that engage many students.

At the beginning of a new century, our challenge is to build on our successes and find creative ways of improving in the less-developed areas. Today, the context for doing campus ministry is more commonly described as postmodern than it was in 1985. The electronic age has arrived in full force. The pace of change is accelerating as we live through one of the greatest transitions in all human history. Social critics specify these changes with words that lack clear content: postcolonial, postindustrial, post-patriarchal, post-denominational, and post-Cold War. Moreover, we face continuing challenges from fundamentalism and secularism as well as new dangers from internal polarization, questionable budget cuts, and unknown consequences of *Ex Corde Ecclesia*, the apostolic constitution issued by Pope John Paul II regarding Catholic colleges and universities on August 15, 1990.

In responding to these contemporary challenges, we are blessed with valuable resources: creative campus ministers who have developed innovative programs; dedicated faculty members and interested students who take seriously the spiritual quest; an expanding pool of trained lay ministers, men and women, who provide solid service to students on a daily basis; affluent Catholics willing to support good programs; and bishops who understand the crucial importance of campus ministry in the life of the church.

We can also draw on the impressive achievements of Catholic theology during the past century (the most productive period since the time of Aquinas and Bonaventure in the thirteenth century), especially the work of the seminal thinkers Karl Rahner, Bernard Lonergan, and Hans Urs von Balthasar, as well as the various liberation theologians who alert us to social sin and the need to empower women, minorities, and all the oppressed.

Effective campus ministers often manifest an intuitive sense that spirituality is the vital dimension and solid ground of all they do—a point that needs more explicit emphasis than found in the pastoral letter. The pressures and failures of daily ministry remind us of our total dependence on the all-powerful God. The challenge of finding our way from the periphery of the academic world to the center turns our attention to Jesus, the marginal Jew, who is the unifying focus of the cosmos. The joys and satisfactions woven into a life of service attune us to the Spirit, who is the source of all blessings. When first published, *Empowered by the Spirit* spoke of a new era and a bright future for campus ministry. Today, eyes of faith, focused by the Spirit, can still detect signs of hope that the future does indeed remain bright with promise.

DIALOGUE WITH FRANCIS

During the last decade and a half, dark clouds have shadowed the bright future for campus ministry. The terrorist attacks of September 11, 2001, on New York and Washington, DC, introduced a vague anxiety that has been intensified by a steady stream of terrorist atrocities around the world, including the downing of a Russian passenger jet and the slaughter of innocent people in Paris. The shooting sprees in schools once considered safe havens have created a sense of radical vulnerability among some collegians. The published reports indicating high rates of rape and sexual assault on campus have revealed the intense suffering of victims and have intensified fears among some women. Advocates for the humanities have found themselves losing ground to those who see college simply as a path to a lucrative job. Some dioceses, usually driven by limited financial resources, have cut back on full-time campus ministers, expecting busy local pastors to minister to the collegians. Some campus ministers feel that the spirit of Vatican II has been lost in the church, while others believe the church on campus is under attack by hostile secular ideologies. Today, it is harder to speak of a future bright with promise than it was at the turn of the century.

For many campus ministers, the pastoral visit of Pope Francis to the United States in September 2015 generated a new sense of optimism. It is helpful to recall some of the events that touched the hearts of so many Americans and reminded Christians of the inherent power of the gospel message to keep hope alive.

In his historic address to the Joint Meeting of Congress, Pope Francis, speaking deliberately in accented English, reminded law makers of their duty "to protect, by means of the law, the image and likeness fashioned by God on every human face." With a brilliant rhetorical move, he raised up the "historical memory" of four Americans: Abraham Lincoln, a great defender of liberty; Martin Luther King Jr., an eloquent spokesman for the dream of justice; Dorothy Day, the social activist dedicated to the care for the poor; and Thomas Merton, the contemplative advocate for dialogue and peace. The reference to Dorothy Day and Thomas Merton drew great praise from Catholics, who see these two inspirational figures as models of a distinctly American spirituality. Veteran observers of Congress reported that they had never seen the members so attentive and moved by a speech of any president or visiting dignitary. The Catholic Speaker of the House, John Boehner, who invited the pope, was visibly moved. Jewish and Protestant senators joined Catholics in glowing praise of Francis as a great moral leader. Caught up in the emotion of the day, some commentators suggested the address would help create a more harmonious and less divisive atmosphere in Congress. Although there is little concrete evidence to support this expectation, it seems important to hold in memory the immediate positive response to the pope as an ongoing reminder of how politicians with real philosophical differences could cooperate for the common good.

Invited to address the seventieth session of the General Assembly of the United Nations, Pope Francis used the occasion to highlight the importance of healthy families and greater educational opportunities for women. He deplored the "modern scourges" of terrorism, human trafficking, the narcotics trade, and the proliferation of weapons, which harm "real men and women." He praised the peacekeeping efforts of the United Nations and indicated his approval of the Iranian nuclear agreement. Echoing his encyclical, *Laudato Si'*, the pope gave special attention to ecological problems created by "the thirst for power and material prosperity." He spoke of a "true right of the environment" based on the fact that humans "live in communion with it" and the conviction that every creature has "an intrinsic value." Arguing his point, Francis noted that all religions believe "the environment is a fundamental good" and that the monotheistic religions believe in a Creator who calls us to respect creation. Applying his fundamental conviction that environmental and human concerns are essentially connected, the pope also spoke out against "the exclusion of the weak and disadvantaged," who are victims of a growing "culture of waste." Mindful of his "grave responsibility" as a religious leader, Francis expressed hope that the international community would make real progress in protecting the environment, starting with the Paris Conference on Climate Change.

There are indications that Francis has changed some minds on environmental issues. The Yale Project on Climate Change Communication released a report on *The Francis Effect: How Pope Francis Changed the Conversation about Global Warming*, indicating that 17 percent of Americans and 35 percent of American Catholics report that Francis influenced their view on global warming. Surveys conducted in March before the release of *Laudato Si'* and in October after the pope's visit to the United States indicate that more Americans (an increase of 4 percent for all Americans and 10 for Catholics) now say global warming is happening; more (an increase of 8 percent for all and 11 for Catholics) are now worried about it; and more now agree with the pope that global warming harms the poor (an increase of 12 percent for all and an amazing 20 percent rise for Catholics from 42 to 62 percent). The report does admit that other causes may be at work but claims that some of these changes must be attributed to Francis.

The pope's speech at the United Nations drew praise from religious and secular sources: Pax Christi USA commended Francis for his "eloquent, simple and direct words" supporting peace through nonviolence; and the *Washington Post* described him as "an inspiration and unrelenting motivator" for protecting the environment and promoting sustainable development.

In introducing Pope Francis to the United Nations' General Assembly, Secretary General Ban Ki-moon referred to his "remarkable global stature as a man of faith among all faiths." With the death of

Nelson Mandela, it seems that Francis is now recognized by many as the premier moral leader in the world. The positive response to his UN speech suggests persons of all faiths as well as nonbelievers are open to perspectives of a religious leader. Remembering that the pope changed some perceptions and attitudes on a crucial topic strengthens our hope that progress can be made on other issues as well.

Each of the pope's speeches had points worth remembering. His speech on religious liberty before Independence Hall in Philadelphia, for example, encouraged Hispanics to treasure their religious heritage and never to be ashamed of their cultural traditions. Delivered in Spanish with great spontaneity and enthusiasm, it revealed the pope's deep compassion for immigrants and can serve as an ongoing reminder of our own responsibilities to the growing number of refugees in our war-torn world.

During his visit, Francis not only interacted with the powerful but also with homeless persons in Washington, DC, the children of immigrants in New York City, and prisoners at a correctional facility on the outskirts of Philadelphia. In those settings, he seemed to come alive and find new energy. His face lit up and his gestures were more animated. He was at home with the kind of persons he served as a priest and bishop in Argentina. To about a hundred young inmates, the pope presented himself as a pastor, "but above all as a brother." His comments were organized around the Last Supper scene in John's Gospel where Jesus washed the feet of his disciples. The journey of life leaves its mark on all of us. We all need cleansing. Jesus wants to heal our wounds, to wash us clean, to restore our dignity, to help us resume the journey and "come back to the table" spread for all. Insisting that "confinement is not the same as exclusion," the pope expressed his personal displeasure with prison systems that "are not concerned to care for wounds" and with those who do not realize that the pain of inmates is also the pain of society. Seeing the world through the eyes of Jesus, we are moved "to create new opportunities for the inmates and their families; for correctional authorities and society as a whole." In a pointed liberating instruction, Francis insisted that Jesus saves us from "the lie that says no one can change."

After his talk, Francis went and greeted each one of the young inmates, blessing some and embracing those who rose from their chairs. Throughout, he exuded a warm, inclusive compassion that clearly touched most, if not all, of the inmates.

It is difficult to know what real effect the prison visit of Francis will have. The United States, which has about 5 percent of the world's population, has 25 percent of the world's prison population, about 2.2 million persons incarcerated. Those passionate about prison reform found great encouragement in the pope's comments. After the papal visit, the Justice Department announced an early release for about 6,000 inmates from federal prisons to reduce overcrowding and to provide relief for drug offenders who received harsh sentences over the past three decades. Although this decision was made independently of Francis, it is in accord with his emphasis on new opportunities for offenders. In early October, several senators, including some Catholics, introduced a criminal justice reform bill designed, in part, to reduce sentences for low-level, nonviolent drug offenders. In supporting the bill, Archbishop Thomas Wenski of Miami, representing the American bishops, cited statements of Pope Francis on prison reform. As our country continues to discuss prison reform, some of us should make sure that the example and teaching of Francis is part of the public debate.

Many of us can recall images of Francis interacting with children, mingling with the homeless, and embracing disabled persons. We remember them as authentic gestures of a genuine human being, a compassionate priest, and an edifying pope who sees himself as a servant of the servants of God. On days when we are tempted to remain imprisoned in our own egocentricity, it may be helpful to recall these images as a stimulus for reaching out to those in need.

This account of the impact of Francis on Americans, in general, and specifically American Catholics, can help campus ministers rekindle the optimistic spirit expressed in *Empowered by the Spirit*, which is still operative in the new millennium. The gospel handed on to us continues to have inherent power to touch the hearts and stimulate the minds of collegians today. For them, as the Canadian philosopher Charles Taylor has reminded us, personal authenticity is an ethical ideal that is in accord with the Christian message (see *The Ethics of Authenticity*). They seem to have an intuitive sense of hypocrisy combined with a respect for honesty and sincerity, which makes them well disposed to Francis and his message. They resonate with the essential message of his encyclical on the environment, although very few have read even parts of it. Campus ministers can use his comments on Dorothy Day and Thomas Merton to introduce students to these saintly individuals who lived authentic Christian lives. The pope's interaction with ordinary people and with those often treated like nonpersons can help young people recognize their inherent worth and develop some sense of their responsibility to help the less fortunate. The visit of Pope Francis and the reports on his activities were uplifting, reminding young people of their own, often forgotten, idealism. The whole visit was a sign of hope for a generation that has known so much violence, confusion, and disruption.

Instructed by Francis, campus ministers who are committed to the spirit of Vatican II can see the students they serve as a sign of hope. This claim is not immediately evident. Catholic millennials attend Mass much less frequently than their grandparents. Some are almost totally socialized into our secular culture, while others pursue spiritual goals without reference to their Catholic heritage. A small percentage can be identified as Catholic fundamentalists who aggressively resist the reforms of Vatican II. Catholic collegians who interact with peers from diverse religious backgrounds tend to develop greater tolerance but also demonstrate a diminished sense of loyalty to their own church. Nevertheless, a case can be made that young American Catholics are a source of hope for those who fear that the reforms of Vatican II will eventually be thwarted by the heirs of the Council minority who want to reform the reform.

According to numerous studies, most Catholic millennials continue to hold the fundamental beliefs of the faith. Over 90 percent believe in God and practice some type of prayer. Around the same percentage affirms the divinity of Christ and believes that at Mass the bread and wine become his body and blood. Their belief in the real presence of Christ is matched by the importance they place on practicing the works of charity. In this regard, the many collegians today who participate in Christian service projects, and include theological reflection in the process, have become valuable carriers of the Catholic social tradition. Despite great challenges, therefore, important core beliefs and practices are still alive among most young adult Catholics in the United States today. We should not let the troubling lack of institutional participation and loyalty among the millennials blind us to the successful and encouraging transmission of core elements of the Catholic heritage to the millennial generation.

Furthermore, Catholic millennials are generally attuned to some important developments fostered by the Second Vatican Council:

for example, the role of the laity, liturgical participation, the value of religious liberty, and the importance of ecumenical and interfaith dialogue. This fascinating alignment is not primarily due to a great catechetical effort to instruct youth in conciliar teaching, although Catholic schools and some religious education programs have made considerable progress in that direction. Most millennials do not have much explicit knowledge of Vatican II and its major teachings. Nor is their own spirituality defined by the debates at the Council. The declining number of Catholics who experienced the pre-Vatican church tend to see themselves as conservatives or liberals, depending on their attitude toward the changes dictated by the Council, especially in the way Mass is celebrated. The next generations were close enough to the shifts in Catholic practices to recognize themselves in terms of the ongoing debate between conservatives and progressives. For most millennials, however, these categories no longer adequately express their own spiritual search and religious journey. It is simply not legitimate or helpful to define them in the terms familiar to their grandparents. Most millennials are not rebelling against a rigid form of Catholic morality that feels suffocating, nor are they, for the most part, rejecting clear doctrinal teaching that contradicts their experience. Their world appears far more amorphous, filled with breakups, fragmentation, chaos, and discontinuity. They have grown up with the threat of international terrorism and random violence in schools. Their spiritual quest, understandably, includes a longing for stability and security. For a minority, this leads to a Catholic fundamentalism that fears the modern, pluralistic world and latches onto elements of the Catholic tradition to fight modernity and fashion a rigid and narrow Catholic identity. Most millennials, however, simply accept the modern world as the given environment for their personal journey through life.

Despite their distance from the dynamics of Vatican II, Catholic millennials feel comfortable with some of its core themes, primarily because they accord with their experience of living in a democratic society and pluralistic culture. The Council, for example, put great emphasis on the church as the people of God. All the baptized share a common dignity as equal members of the Body of Christ. The laity share in the responsibility of spreading the reign of God in the world. They have the right and obligation to share their views with their pastors. These themes, often summarized in the statement "we are the church," resonate well with millennial Catholics in the United States and other democratic countries. When young Catholics participate in any organization, including the church, they expect to have their voices heard. They tend to reject arbitrary uses of authority, and are more at home with democratic procedures, open dialogue, and shared decision-making. Pastors who function as authentic servant leaders can gain the respect and cooperation of millennial Catholics, who have a culturally conditioned resistance to clerical authoritarianism.

The Council insisted that liturgy is communal worship and that conscious, active participation in the Mass is the expected norm for all members of the worshiping community. It seems that this part of the reform initiated by the Council has taken hold among young Catholics. They generally recognize that the liturgy is common worship and not simply for private prayer. The liturgical changes have encouraged this outlook: singing together, sharing the greeting of peace, assuming common postures, and saying the prayers together in the vernacular. Not all millennials who attend Mass regularly participate fully, but most realize they are involved in a common act of worship.

Basing its teaching on the dignity of persons and gospel values, the Council's *Declaration on Religious Liberty* declared that persons and religious communities have a right to religious freedom. All people should have the freedom to worship according to their own conscience and to practice their religion if this does not interfere with public order. The church does not seek a privileged position in society but does require freedom to carry out its mission in the world. The state should guarantee religious liberty by constitutional law. These points seem familiar and obvious to Catholics in the United States, including millennials. Most simply assume that tolerance toward other religions is a good thing and that religious liberty is a right for all. Young Catholics have not experienced the kind of anti-Catholic prejudice endured by older generations, and they feel no need to seek a privileged position in society. It is difficult to convince most of them that the Catholic community is under attack from the political establishment and the secular media. Furthermore, the claim that religious freedom necessarily leads to relativism and indifference does not ring true to most Catholic millennials.

Vatican II encouraged dialogue and cooperation among Christian denominations and the world religions. Catholics, open to the truth and goodness in other religions, can enter this dialogue with confidence in their own tradition. Millennial collegians who get to know

85

students from other religions tend to be more open to dialogue and collaboration on projects of common interest. They are less receptive to suggestions that salvation is limited to Catholics and more in tune with the salvation optimism taught by the Council.

As this summary suggests, we now have a considerable number of young Catholics who not only resonate with major conciliar developments, but are also grounded in traditional church teaching on God, Christ, real presence, and social justice. Furthermore, they are instinctively, if not explicitly, opposed to the kind of clericalism and exclusivism advocated by those who continue to resist the spirit and explicit statements of the Council. Millennial Catholics, even with their serious shortcomings, can still serve as a sign of hope for those committed to the spirit of the Second Vatican Council. With proper guidance from campus ministers, they can be great allies for Pope Francis and his reform projects.

III

PERSONS WHO SERVE ON CAMPUS

5

MILLENNIAL SPIRITUALITY

The pastoral letter notes the responsibility of all baptized persons on campus to help higher education reach its potential and to build up the faith community. To assist this effort, professional campus ministers have the task of identifying, developing, and coordinating the diverse gifts of the members of the church on campus, including administrators, faculty members, and students, both traditional-aged and older. To achieve this, they need to know the people they serve, their interests and passions, their joys and sorrows, their strengths and weaknesses, their theological perspectives and spiritual practices.

This chapter focuses on the spirituality of traditional-aged collegians and how this impacts campus ministry programming. The main points remain valid and useful, but it is also important to consider more current trends. According to well-publicized reports by the Pew Research Center, young Catholics in the United States are leaving the church at a high rate, with only 16 percent of millennials identifying themselves as Catholics compared to 24 percent of all adults. Numerous studies have indicated that students beginning college in 2015 are having more emotional problems than in past years, with more than half reporting "overwhelming anxiety and about one third experiencing frequent depression." These studies suggest that students are working harder and socializing less, which is affecting their emotional stability. Millennial collegians are increasingly dependent on social media for connecting with others and for news and information. According to a study done at Baylor University, collegians spend as many as nine hours a day on their cell phones with approximately 60 percent admitting they may be addicted to their phones. On an average day, they spend over ninety minutes texting, forty-eight minutes checking Facebook, and thirty-four minutes surfing the internet. Since the creation of Facebook in 2004 and Twitter in 2008, collegians have increasingly used social media as a primary means of communicating with others. The internet gives them instant access to vast stores of information, which they use to do research for their papers. They depend on their smart phones to accompany them through the day: catching up on the news; accessing the internet wherever they are; texting friends; calling their parents; getting help in emergencies; and locating the next party scene.

Critics of social media focus on the way they hinder the development of healthy personal relationships. Students who spend many hours by themselves on the internet miss many chances to interact with their peers. Addiction to social media can blind collegians to their responsibilities to their parents and to the cultural and social opportunities on campus. Texting can be a substitute for face-to-face meetings and an escape from challenging encounters. Some critics claim that collegians who spend so much time in the virtual world are becoming more self-centered and less responsive to the needs of others in the real world. We need further scholarly research to get a more accurate and comprehensive understanding of how the latest cohort of millennials is affected by the omnipresence of social media. Whatever the results of such studies, campus ministers must find creative ways to help students grow spiritually and to encourage their participation in the mission of the church. The following material, which draws on sociological studies as well as my own research, was first presented at a campus ministers' conference at Notre Dame in June of 2004, and provides important background material for meeting that responsibility.

THE SPIRITUALITY OF CONTEMPORARY YOUNG ADULTS

Campus ministers have the challenge of assisting young adults' move through the transitions from high school to college and beyond. These transitions have a spiritual dimension that can be described in both religious and secular terms. Christian spirituality involves submitting to the will of God the Father, putting on the mind of Christ, and being attentive to the prompting of the Holy Spirit. Authentic spirituality has a communal character that suggests co-responsibility for the church, active participation in the liturgy, and collaboration in the work of justice and peace. The spiritual quest seeks reconciling relationships with God, other human beings, the whole of nature, and our true selves. The word *spirituality* points to the depth dimension of all human experience and to the Mystery that sustains and encompasses human existence. In more secular terms, spirituality is concerned with the search for meaning amid absurdity, commitment in a society of open options, purpose in an aimless world, depth in a superficial culture, and integration in a fragmented existence.

For campus ministry, discussion of spirituality raises challenging, practical questions. How can we help collegians pray with greater devotion, get more out of scripture, integrate more completely love of God and neighbor, participate more actively in the liturgy, and live their faith more fully in everyday life? Put in more secular language, how can we help them maintain an inner peace in a stressful world, find their vocation in life, contribute to the common good, and work for peace and justice in the world? In helping collegians develop a viable spirituality, what theological framework guides our efforts and what programs, practices, activities, and strategies work best?

RESOURCES

In helping collegians manage transitions, Catholic campus ministers have been guided for decades by the bishops' pastoral letter *Empowered by the Spirit*. Effective ministers have found creative ways of adapting the general principles in this document to the needs of their students. The sociological studies of young adults, such as *Young Adult Catholics: Religion in the Culture of Choices* by Dean Hoge et al. and *The Search for Common Ground* by James Davidson, provide helpful data, as does my personal interaction with students over almost thirty-five years of serving in university parishes. Over those years, I have been impressed with the great creative ministry offered on campuses throughout the United States and have tried to tap that great fund of practical wisdom. Recently, about thirty of my students who participate in our Christian Leadership Program filled out an extensive questionnaire on transitions and spirituality. It is not a scientific survey, but it suggests how our best Catholic students manage these transitions. As a Catholic pastor and a theologian heavily influenced by the German Jesuit, Karl Rahner, my hope is that my personal experience will be helpful to others.

91

INFLUENCES

Students entering college at the beginning of the new millennium reflect the influence of various spiritual, religious, and cultural factors. These millennials, as they are sometimes called, have the same spiritual longings as previous generations for meaning and purpose in life. They must contend with the essential conflict between their infinite longings and their finite capabilities. Their challenges sound familiar to all campus ministers: forming their personal identity; developing good friendships; finding a life partner; choosing a career; appropriating their religious heritage; cultivating habits of good citizenship; and deciding how to relate to the dominant culture. In my dealings with collegians, I have been more impressed with the similarities among generations than the differences. Human nature is common. Millennials still fall in love and empathize with suffering loved ones. It is more important for campus ministers to understand the spiritual character of human existence than to know the latest popular songs.[1]

As with previous generations, collegians today are influenced by their parents and family life. They are, however, more likely to come from broken homes and are less likely to experience the sense of security provided by a stable loving family. Some studies suggest that they are closer to their parents than previous generations, more demanding of a secure environment on campus, and more respectful of social conventions and institutions.[2] Reflecting on discussions with my students, I am impressed with how often they refer to one of their parents in a positive way as a role model, a spiritual guide, a confidant, or a friend. Some universities are responding to this trend by appealing more directly to parents.

American culture continues to exercise enormous influence on millennial collegians, often at a preconscious level. Some cultural trends, such as rugged individualism, unbridled hedonism, lavish consumerism, and uncritical nationalism, are anti-gospel and harmful to healthy spiritual growth. Other ideals, including authenticity, self-actualization, freedom, and volunteerism, when placed in a Christian framework, can promote healthy spiritual development. Collegians grow up in a country where most citizens believe in God, pray periodically, and are affiliated with a religious organization. The Christian entertainment industry generates over $3 billion a year in movies, concerts, and books. During the last four years of the twentieth century, polls indicated that interest in spirituality among teenagers increased almost 25 percent, a trend that anecdotal evidence suggests is continuing. Our culture is an ambivalent mix of secular and religious currents.[3]

For the most part, the richly textured Catholic subculture that shaped Catholic spirituality in the past has largely disappeared, although remnants remain in predominately Catholic areas where the parish is still the prime socializing institution. I have a few students from rural Ohio who come from intact Catholic families, went to Catholic schools for twelve years, have only Catholic friends and relatives, and live with the assumption that you go to Mass every Sunday. Most of my students, however, have gleaned fragments of their spirituality from various sources, including parish liturgies, youth retreats, and religious education classes. Those who attended Catholic high schools have at least been exposed to resources that can help to integrate these diverse spiritual elements.

Millennial collegians are living through one of the great transition periods of human history as we move from the modern to the postmodern world.[4] They are developing their fundamental spiritual outlook in a world that is post-patriarchal, post-denominational, post-industrial, post-colonial, and post-Cold War. Their consciousness and very mode of processing information is shaped by the electronic age of television, computers, and the internet. Millennial collegians often manifest characteristics of the premodern and modern world as well as the postmodern. An individual student may, for example, simultaneously hold a naïve premodern literal interpretation of the Bible, maintain a modern trust in science and technology as the sole instrument of human progress, and function with an unexamined postmodern assumption that any absolute-truth claims are absurd and oppressive. All collegians today deal with transitions in their personal lives in the larger context of a world characterized more by change than stability.

Millennials carry vivid images of the Columbine shooting spree and the terrorist attacks of September 11, 2001. From an early age, they have lived in a world threatened by random, unpredictable violence. Some commentators believe this has produced a sense of "radical vulnerability" that can lead to a greater awareness of absolute dependence on God. Other scholars have noted that collegians now seldom talk about September 11 and already show diminished interest in the annual campus commemoration of the terrorist attack. Pearl Harbor directly affected the daily life of everyone in the United

States, and the assassination of President Kennedy eventually led many into the civil rights movement. It has been much easier, except for air travel, for the millennial generation to go on with life as usual after September 11, 2001.

GOALS FOR CAMPUS MINISTRY

In the broadest terms, campus ministry has the goal of helping collegians become better disciples of Christ, more attuned to the will of God, and more effective vehicles of the Spirit. We want graduates of our programs to take seriously their baptismal call to holiness and their task of spreading the reign of God in the world. They should be serious about developing a rich interior life nourished by private prayer and meditation as well as regular and active participation in the liturgy. Well-formed collegians will have a relational spirituality that enables them to establish good marriages, sustain healthy friendships, and cooperate with colleagues in the workplace. Their spirituality will be communal, prompting them to function as responsible citizens, good neighbors, active parishioners, and effective participants in voluntary associations. They will bring a sense of dedication, joy, and hope to their life in the church and society.

In guiding collegians to a more mature spirituality, campus ministers must respond to the specific challenges of the contemporary world. One of our important tasks is to overcome the unfortunate split between spirituality and religion, which contributes to the private spirituality prevalent in our culture.[5] While *spirituality* is generally a positive word today, institutional religion carries negative connotations of rigid authoritarianism and stifling hierarchical power. We must demonstrate to our students that the doctrines, creeds, rituals, and laws of the Christian religion have an inherent power to make us wiser, more fulfilled, and more loving persons. Christianity provides a solid foundation for the spiritual quest and powerful motivation for pursuing it wholeheartedly. Students consciously pursuing spiritual growth will get more out of their religious activities. Institutional religion and spirituality are not essentially opposed, but are components of an integrated human life. An authentic Christian spirituality is necessarily ecclesial.

Campus ministers also have the challenging task of grounding spirituality in a solid theological foundation. Religious illiteracy is a major problem in the culture and clearly affects the millennials. When spirituality is divorced from theology, it is in danger of becoming faddish, superficial, and unbalanced. Collegians who rely on the popular self-help books for spiritual guidance are in danger of neglecting the social dimension of spirituality. An untutored ecumenical spirituality is tempted to neglect the concrete particularity of various traditions while settling for a lowest common denominator. Catholic students who know little about the Bible and modern biblical criticism are often easy prey for aggressive fundamentalists. Collegians passionate about social justice, but unacquainted with Catholic social teaching, can drift into a merely horizontal spirituality that neglects private and liturgical prayer. Students nourished by their small faith-sharing communities, which lack an adequate ecclesiology, can forget that they are part of a larger church. Millennials who have maintained a strong sacramental sense of life may remain stuck in a false consciousness that neglects social sin, institutional evil, and systemic injustice.

Campus ministers can assist students dealing with these concerns by giving due attention to the practice of appropriating the faith. We must help students overcome religious illiteracy and gain a more mature understanding of their faith. Solid catechesis is crucial to healthy spiritual development. Theology is our ally in the task. As Karl Rahner once claimed, the more scientific theology is, the more spiritually relevant it will be. We want our students to see their Christian faith as a valuable resource for understanding the great questions of meaning, purpose, and identity and for living as responsible, mature persons. Our graduates should be committed to a lifelong process of appropriating the faith so that they can grow ever closer to Christ. Adopting the terminology of Jacques Maritain, they need not only "tender hearts" that reflect the compassion of Jesus, but also "tough minds" that enable them to apply Christian principles to complex situations. They should come to see their Christian faith as a synthesis of comprehensive, organic wisdom and not as a disparate collection of doctrines, rituals, and laws. Christianity is a total way of life, an integrated symbol system with a clear focus on commitment to Christ, the definitive prophet and absolute savior.

In addition to these fundamental attitudes, we want our Catholic collegians to gain a variety of theological skills: to read scripture intelligently; to defend their faith against both secularists and fundamentalists; to engage in theological reflection that relates their faith to everyday life; to find unity in the midst of great pluralism in the church; to participate in ecumenical and interfaith dialogue and collaboration; to appreciate the distinctive characteristics of Catholicism, especially the sacramental principle; and to know how to use resources such as the *Catechism of the Catholic Church*, biblical commentaries, and the documents of Vatican II for answering questions as they arise.

Graduates of our campus ministry programs should have acquired specific information about various aspects of their faith: the Bible, including its meaning and interpretation; the broad outline of church history; the spirit and various teachings of the Second Vatican Council; the main themes of Catholic social teaching; the major saints and spiritual masters; the great theologians; and the fundamental themes of contemporary theology. These attitudes, skills, and knowledge are essential for the development of a viable, balanced spirituality.

Spiritual growth involves a process of developing virtues that enable us to act habitually like Christ in changing circumstances. We want to assist our students in the task of growing in the theological virtues of faith, hope, and charity and the moral virtues of prudence, temperance, fortitude, and justice. To function efficiently in the postmodern world, collegians are well served by what we might call "dialectical virtues," which enable them to keep opposed tendencies in fruitful tension.[6] The dialectical virtue of committed openness, for example, provides them with the facility to be so committed to their Catholic faith that they are open to truth, goodness, and beauty wherever they are found. Hopeful realism prompts them to avoid both a naïve optimism and a cynical pessimism while finding signs of hope in embracing the reality of life. Reflective spontaneity encourages them to maintain a regular regimen of prayer that grounds wholehearted engagement in the present moment. Enlightened simplicity moves collegians to ongoing study of their faith so they can be more Christlike in their daily lives. We want our graduates to be prayerfully prophetic Christians who are nourished by private and liturgical prayer for the arduous work of creating a more just and peaceful world.

Students associated with various spiritual interests have specific needs. The goal is to help them build on their strengths and rise above their limitations. Those overwhelmed by busyness or guilt need to get in touch with the eclipsed spiritual longings of their hearts. Those on a private spiritual journey need positive experiences of church whereby institutional religion can enrich their spiritual quest. Helping ecumenical Catholics develop stronger institutional loyalty is a difficult but worthy goal. Fundamentalist Catholics need to learn that their ultimate security is in the faithful God and not in a rigid, closed Catholic identity. Catholics with a communal spirituality must remember their connection with the larger church. Those with a prophetic spirituality need reminders to nourish their passion for justice by private and liturgical prayer. Catholics who see the world as sacramental often need a stronger sense of social sin. Campus ministry programs should have the general goal of meeting the spiritual needs of diverse groups of students.

PRACTICES, PROGRAMS, STRATEGIES

Since its publication in 1985, *Empowered by the Spirit* has encouraged Catholic campus ministers to organize their programming around six practices or ministerial functions: forming community, appropriating the faith, facilitating personal development, forming the Christian conscience, educating for justice and peace, and developing future leaders. These practices have a spiritual dimension and each one contributes to the general goal of helping students develop an integrated, balanced spirituality rooted in the Catholic tradition.

FORMING COMMUNITY

For most Catholic campus ministry programs, the eucharistic liturgy is the key to forming community and developing a healthy spirituality. Students growing up without a Catholic subculture depend on the liturgy for their sense of Catholic identity. Regular participation in the Eucharist inculcates the sacramental sense of human existence and prompts efforts to bring greater justice to our world. Students who help plan liturgies get more out of them. They generally prefer music that is lively, upbeat, and singable and homilies that relate the scriptures to their everyday experiences. Special liturgies throughout the year can gather larger crowds and demonstrate the power of the Eucharist to create a sense of community. One of our most successful liturgies is a pre-Christmas Mass on the Sunday before finals that draws large crowds and even brings alumni back to Corpus Christi University Parish. The students invest much time and effort planning the liturgy, which often includes liturgical dance and special proclamations of the Scripture readings. The liturgy taps the Christmas spirit and celebrates the end of the semester. The Second Vatican Council taught that the liturgy is the font and summit of the Christian life. At our pre-Christmas Mass, students experience the inherent power of the Eucharist to nourish a healthy spirituality.

Reaching out to collegians whose spiritual impulses are blunted or eclipsed is a great challenge to campus ministers. We can help them indirectly by cooperating with the university in creating a campus community that embodies high ethical standards and human values.[7] A variety of cooperative efforts are possible: for example, programs to combat binge drinking, credit card debt, sexual promiscuity, classroom cheating, and substance abuse. Campus ministers should lead the way in challenging the widespread and destructive pattern of "work and spend," which traps collegians in an insidious cycle of working more hours to have more consumer goods.

More direct approaches are also needed to minister to this group. Following the advice of a local advertising firm based on focus group data, our parish puts significant effort into getting students' names and contacting them during the first two weeks of the new academic year. Our students go around campus on golf carts giving away free goods, such as mugs and sweatshirts, and getting individuals to sign up for a raffle of a bicycle or DVD player. The parish provides free breakfasts, entertainment, and other inducements to get these students to come to our facility. During the summer before school begins, we make an earnest effort to get the names of Catholic freshmen so that our students can write them a personal letter inviting them to our parish services and activities. All this effort is based on the idea that collegians make decisions in their first weeks on campus that affect their spirituality for the next four years.

Our parish also sponsors small faith-sharing groups in each residence hall on campus with the explicit purpose of reaching out to the inactive Catholics. They read and discuss the Scripture readings for the following week. Active members accept the responsibility to seek out inactive Catholics and personally invite them to the weekly discussions. The group also meets on Sundays and walks over together to the church for Mass. We find that collegians often come to our programs in groups and that many students find it hard to come alone. Even my more mature students report that as freshmen they felt insecure, afraid of the unknown, lost in a large university, doubtful about making friends, and worried about what others think of them. Our parish provided them with an opportunity to meet other students with similar values, to get involved in a structured organization, and to use their gifts to serve others. Thanks to the blessings of a vital faith community, these students say they grew spiritually, coming closer to Christ and learning to love themselves and others.

Echoing the common experience around the country, our students have found that retreats led by peers are one of the most effective ways to overcome isolation, building community and promoting spiritual growth. Forming community in this and other creative ways is critical to the spiritual formation of collegians today.

APPROPRIATING THE FAITH

At our university parish, we place a great emphasis on appropriating the faith as the basis for solid spiritual growth. We continually repeat the message that collegians cannot function in today's world with a high school understanding of their faith. They need a more mature faith that can deal with the challenges of the postmodern world.

To this end, Corpus Christi University Parish worked with the University of Toledo, a state university, in establishing a Chair of Catholic Studies. We collected an endowment of $1.5 million and gave it to the university under a contractual agreement that a recognized scholar on the Catholic tradition would be hired as a tenured faculty member to teach two courses each semester on some aspect of the Catholic tradition. In conjunction with this initiative, we encouraged other religious traditions to establish their own professorships or chairs and worked with the university to establish a religious studies major. The chair, now held by the outstanding Catholic ecclesiologist Richard Gaillardetz, has worked extremely well. He has brought the Catholic perspective to important public discussions on campus and in the community. His courses have been well attended and the number of religious studies majors has increased. This year alone, five students from our parish have chosen to go on to graduate studies in theology or religious studies at fine schools including the University of Notre Dame, Boston College, and the Catholic Theological Union in Chicago.

At our parish, we try to supplement the courses on campus with our own programs: regular Bible study, independent studies on religious topics, and periodic seminars on current topics, such as Mel Gibson's movie,

99

The Passion of the Christ, or the sex-abuse scandal in the church. Each semester, we run a series of six lectures by prominent theologians from around the country on several topics including scripture, theology, and spirituality. These efforts to help our students appropriate their faith help set a foundation for a spirituality that avoids fads and reflects the long and rich Catholic tradition.

DEVELOPING LEADERS

Another major initiative of Corpus Christi is our Christian Leadership Program, which offers theological education, leadership training, and spiritual formation over a four-year period for selected Catholic students at the University of Toledo. The goal is to prepare leaders for the church and society who are solidly grounded in their Catholic tradition. Twelve students are selected by a committee each year to receive $5,000 scholarships and are required to take classes and assume leadership positions. During their first year, they take my credit course that is a popular version of Karl Rahner's *Foundations of Christian Faith*. In the second year, six experts in leadership lead a series of discussions designed to give students practical skills. In the last two years, the students assume leadership positions in the parish and on campus and write theological reflection papers on their experiences.

We need leaders in the church and society who are not only dedicated but also firmly rooted in their Catholic tradition. Students graduating from this program are well prepared to serve on parish councils, liturgy committees, social justice action groups, and other parish organizations. After completion of the program, the students receive certification that will facilitate their participation in their new parishes.

The initial success in producing excellent student leaders (one served as President of Student Government and another as Chair of the National Catholic Student Association) provides hope that this program will indeed help prepare graduates for future leadership positions in church and society.

One of the delights of this program is the gradual development of students over a four-year period. Their personal stories, their struggles, and their progress toward greater Christian maturity are inspiring. Statistical reports about collegians take on a human face through my close interactions with these select students.

OTHER PRACTICES

Our parish is also involved with the other ministerial practices outlined in the pastoral letter. Providing spiritual direction for students is an important part of facilitating their personal development. Our student retreat each year provides students with an opportunity to interact daily with a spiritual director over a five-day period. We run a series of "pairing programs" that put collegians into contact with members of our permanent parish community. For example, we pair a student with a faculty member and ask them to meet three times a semester outside the classroom setting. We also make connections according to career choices; for instance, pairing an engineering student with a practicing engineer. These interactions, which facilitate personal development, have a spiritual dimension that can be made more explicit through theological reflection and discussion.

We have found that our social justice activities, such as Habitat Spring Break, are more beneficial spiritually when we gather for prayer ahead of time and spend time in theological reflection afterward.

Homilies provide a wonderful opportunity for conscience formation. This is especially true if preachers address the personal issues that interest students, such as premarital sex, as well as the more public issues of justice and peace.

These few examples suggest that *Empowered by the Spirit* provides a useful framework for strategies, practices, and programs that can assist the spiritual growth of our students. These practices work especially well when geared to the specific needs of students.

LEAVING COLLEGE

Students leaving college and embarking on a career face numerous spiritual challenges: carving out time for prayer amid busy lives; finding meaning in their work; balancing work and leisure; combating destructive cultural trends, such as individualism, hedonism, and consumerism; establishing a healthy family; working for greater justice in society; and living as good citizens. To function as effective Christians, graduates need a local parish to sustain and guide them. They also need role models, individuals who find God in ordinary life and bring Christian principles to the marketplace and political arena.

Campus ministers should think in terms of helping prepare graduates for life in the world. They need to recognize that family and career offer new opportunities to grow spiritually. The spiritual journey is lifelong and leads eventually to the transition into eternal life. The virtues developed in college should help graduates act as Christians in new and complex situations.

Marriage preparation programs that draw on the experience and wisdom of married couples are helpful to the collegians who take them seriously. The habit of applying the lessons of the weekly liturgies to student life can also carry over to life in the world.

Campus ministers should remind students of their responsibility to take what they learned in campus faith communities to their new parishes. They need encouragement to stay loyal to their religious tradition. Many Catholic graduates will shop around for a parish they like. They are in a supermarket situation where there is competition among denominations for new members. Some may be willing to stay with a Catholic parish that is less fulfilling to try and make it better. We expect the graduates of our Christian Leadership Program to use their training in constructive ways to build up local parishes.

At the end of the academic year, Corpus Christi University Parish has a special liturgy celebrating the blessings of the year and the challenges ahead. We honor the graduating seniors and have one of them give a witness talk on what the parish has meant to him or her. This usually includes expressions of gratitude to the permanent members of the parish who teach marriage courses, participate in our pairing programs, and during the academic year, feed the students every Sunday after the 6:00 p.m. Mass. The homily at that Mass encourages the graduates to be lights to the world, to share what they have learned with others. This farewell liturgy reminds us that our graduates are on a continuing spiritual journey. Our hope is that they find guidance and nourishment from their Catholic heritage as they make yet another life transition with its distinctive challenges and opportunities.

DIALOGUE WITH FRANCIS

The pope encourages campus ministers to accompany students on their life journey with its major transitions. It is important to recognize the common spiritual elements in their journey as well as the specific challenges of their postmodern world. In this regard, Francis offers a helpful critique of social media. The concluding chapter of

Laudato Si' treats the "digital world" in the section on the decline in the quality of human life (n. 47). Although he acknowledges the "exciting possibilities" offered by social media in "sharing knowledge and affections," the pope emphasizes the destructive tendencies of the "digital world," which can prevent persons from "learning how to live wisely, to think deeply, and to love generously." The "information overload" can block out "the great sages of the past" and replace real relationships with other people, leaving us with "a sort of mental pollution." Social media can shield us from "direct contact with the pain, the fears, and the joys of others and the complexity of their personal experiences," leading to a "melancholic dissatisfaction with interpersonal relations, or a harmful sense of isolation." We achieve wisdom not by accumulating data, but by reflection, dialogue, and personal encounters. Once again recognizing their potential for good, the pope encourages us to "help these media become sources of new cultural progress for humanity."

Campus ministers who work with students immersed in the digital world have a special responsibility to help them use social media wisely. This includes some warnings: do not presume that every Catholic website is in tune with the teachings and spirit of Vatican II; do not post any personal information that could be embarrassing in future situations, such as a job interview; be careful not to share material that is confidential or that can hurt others; beware of becoming addicted to the internet or spending too much time on it; do not use cell phones to text during class or to cheat on exams; do not assume that everything on the internet is true; beware of the seductive power of pornographic material so readily available on the internet; do not interrupt conversations with friends to make calls on your cell phone; do not let social media substitute for face-to-face encounters with family and friends. On the positive side, campus ministers can encourage student efforts to use social media to further the mission of the church on campus: advertising events; eliciting ideas for new programs; staying in touch with parents; posting helpful quotes from classic theological works and popular spiritual writers. In looking for creative approaches, we should note that Pope Francis has a Twitter account that reaches over 20 million followers and has almost ten million retweets. We should also note that the pope is cautious about social media, refusing to go on Facebook because, according to a Vatican official, negative responses would be available for the world to see. Thus, Francis encourages campus ministers to use social media creatively but also prudently.

In his various addresses to young persons, Francis consistently challenges them to live their faith with courage, joy, and hope. He encourages them to embrace Christ's law of love and to rebel against a culture that reduces love to its sexual aspect, depriving it of "its essential characteristics of beauty, communion, fidelity and responsibility." In his homily for the 2013 World Youth Day in Rio de Janeiro, Francis called upon his "young friends" to go and proclaim Christ to the world and to do so with courage and in a spirit of serving others. Francis presents the life of courageous service as the way for young persons to find happiness and fulfillment, something that all seek.

Campus ministers tutored by Francis strive to create a missionary community of faith that reaches out to students who are hurting in numerous ways: burdened with alienation and depression that affects so many; addicted to the internet; caught up in the hook-up culture that separates sex from love; attracted to a secular mind-set that denies the mystery dimension of life; and limited by systemic injustice.

To apply the well-known image of Francis, the leaders of the church on campus should establish "a field hospital" mentality, which encourages all those who gather for worship to look for ways to help students wounded in these and other ways. For example: staff members can be more attentive to those lost in the university structure; counselors can help them deal with emotional problems; faculty can offer encouragement to those struggling academically; students can befriend peers who feel alienated. Inspired by Pope Francis, all the baptized can serve in the field hospital that is the church on campus.

6

PROFESSIONAL
CAMPUS MINISTERS

The third section of *Empowered by the Spirit* focuses on the professional campus ministers, the men and women trained to lead the faith community on campus. One of their "most important functions" is to articulate a compelling vision that encourages all the baptized to work together for the well-being of the academic community and the church on campus. The bishops, writing in 1985, saw the growing numbers of laypeople serving on campus as "a sign of hope" and recognized the "historical significance" of the expanded leadership opportunities for women "who in the past have not always been allowed to take their proper role in the Church's ministry" (n. 25). The bishops encouraged the formation of team ministries that pray together and combine talents in a cooperative effort to support the church on campus. They also encourage campus ministers to take responsibility for their own spiritual and professional development, which will enable them to be more effective role models for students and faculty members. The bishops concluded their treatment of professional campus ministers with a strong statement of support: "We recognize our responsibility as bishops to offer all campus ministers moral support, to provide financial assistance to the degree this is needed and possible, and to help them achieve the competency they need to be effective witnesses of the Gospel" (n. 32). The following material was presented as advice for beginning campus ministers. It can also serve as a helpful reminder for more experienced ministers.

ADVICE FOR CAMPUS MINISTERS

These practical suggestions for new campus ministers will hope-fully prompt some self-critical reflection among us veterans as well. Each of the suggestions is placed in a developmental framework, rec-ognizing that spiritual growth is a process, and each contains a coun-terpoint designed to avoid imbalances.

1. *Develop a comprehensive view of campus ministry while recog-nizing personal limitations.* The bishops' pastoral letter, *Empowered by the Spirit*, provides a helpful overview of six ministerial practices: Forming the Faith Community, Appropriating the Faith, Forming the Christian Conscience, Educating for Justice, Facilitating Personal Growth, and Developing Leaders for the Future. Each of these min-isterial practices can enhance both the academic community and the faith community. Furthermore, all six may be used to serve various groups, including administrators, faculty, students, and ourselves as ministers. For example, campus ministry programs can help the uni-versity become a just, open, purposeful, caring, disciplined, and cel-ebrative community that supports the emotional, moral, intellectual, and religious development of faculty, staff, and students. Since the six ministerial practices are so fundamental, they form a comprehensive grid for planning, executing, and evaluating a campus ministry pro-gram as well as the service of individual ministers.

At the same time, no program, team, or individual can attend fully to this vast array of ministerial tasks. The grid is designed to suggest pos-sibilities, not to foster guilt feelings or a sense of inadequacy. It is espe-cially important for new ministers to achieve a realistic view of what they can be and accomplish. Positively, it is possible to use the six ministerial practices to evaluate performances and to plan for future developments. For example, a team might recognize that their retreats are doing an excellent job of forming a faith community, but more effort must be put into helping faculty members appropriate the faith. A newcomer to a ministry team could examine how her talents and interests match or expand the current practices. Those beginning in campus ministry are well advised to read the pastoral letter to gain an overview and then concentrate on one practice, such as forming the faith community. After a year of experience, attending the Frank J. Lewis summer institute pro-vides a terrific opportunity to plan next steps.

2. Develop confidence while maintaining a proper humility. It is easy to imagine a new campus minister facing a crisis of confidence — overwhelmed by responsibilities, unfamiliar with the academic world, intimidated by powerful administrators, overmatched by scholarly professors, and unprepared to meet the needs of students. Veteran campus ministers recognize elements of this crisis and can add their own list of experiences that foster feelings of inadequacy: for example, interacting with academics who patronize us and consider religion either dehumanizing or irrelevant.

Given this situation, campus ministers need confidence that we have a significant role to play and an important message to deliver. Our confidence is ultimately rooted in our calling to be ambassadors on the campus of Christ, who is the Word of God, the Wisdom of the Father, the Icon of Divine Truth. We represent the great Catholic tradition that has distinctive resources for countering questionable tendencies in the university culture: our communal sense of human existence challenges various forms of individualism; our commitment to asceticism counters the destructive elements of consumerism; our liturgical practices challenge the presuppositions of rationalism; our natural law teaching offers an alternative to doctrinaire relativism; our respect for tradition challenges elements of the postmodern culture; and our rich heritage of spirituality exposes the limitations of a one-dimensional world. In this regard, we can speak of a Catholic moment, a time in history when the distinctive resources of the Catholic tradition provide an antidote for what ails the academic world.

The significance of campus ministry also appears when we reflect on our opportunities to interact with students during an especially important, formative time of their lives. Collegians are working out their identity, learning how to relate to others, searching for a life partner, discerning their vocation, developing an internal moral compass, and appropriating their received faith. We interact with students who enjoy a new freedom and need help coping with moral temptations and intellectual challenges to their faith. We are with them as they gain confidence, make friends, fall in love, prepare for a career, and deepen their spiritual life. The sociologists tell us that the personal progress made by students during their collegiate years is a great predictor of how they will be and behave in later life. It is a great blessing for campus ministers to be involved in such a significant process.

In addition to grasping intellectually the importance of campus ministry, we need prayerful reflection to help build and solidify our confidence. We do well to meditate on the historical Jesus, who spoke with absolute authority, and on our Catholic heritage, which is a rich countercultural resource. It is healthy to offer prayers of thanksgiving for ministerial successes: inspiring liturgies, beneficial Christian service projects, Spirit-filled retreats, effective marriage preparation programs, solid spiritual direction, and wise counseling.

Daily prayers of gratitude help us not only to focus on the positive side of ministry but also to cultivate the virtue of humility. We say that humility is truth and we can think of prayer as a form of truth-telling. Prayer instructs us in fundamental truths: we are totally dependent on God; we share in Christ's saving work; and we are empowered by the Spirit. Given the daunting challenges facing campus ministry, our emphasis must be on building confidence, but always in the context of humble dependence on God.

3. *Develop a respect for the academic world while maintaining a critical distance.* Effective campus ministers feel at home in academia and have a fundamental respect for its highest ideals: the pursuit of truth, the quest for wisdom, the acceptance of pluralism, the importance of civil discourse, the respect for persons, the goal of self-actualization, and the value of community service. New campus ministers who harbor subtle feelings of arrogant disdain for the academic world or tend to see the university as an alien territory filled with enticing temptations will have trouble dialoguing and collaborating with groups and individuals on campus. Campus ministers should cultivate a mutually critical, respectful, and enriching dialogue with the university and its members. Each partner can learn from the other and both can cooperate for the common good. In the ongoing conversation, campus ministers have Christ and the gospel as criteria for judging positive and negative trends in the academic community.

Campus ministry cannot allow itself to be relegated to the margins of the academic world. It is impossible to be leaven for a community from the outside. We have a ministry to the university as well as to those believers who constitute the community of faith. Newcomers to campus ministry can employ many strategies for getting more involved in the academic world: read the campus newspaper, befriend a faculty or staff member, serve on a university committee, teach a class or take one, meet students for lunch in the cafeteria, cosponsor an event on campus that deals with religion or ethical questions, and be available as a guest lecturer in a class. All of us can learn from veteran campus ministers who have moved to the center of the academic world in more dramatic ways: establishing working relationships with high-level administrators and senior faculty members; getting ethics courses started in various departments; promoting a religious studies department or major; and establishing Chairs of Catholic Studies.

4. *Develop a flexible spiritual regimen while maintaining a life of wholehearted service.* Campus ministry tends to be all-consuming. Newcomers have much to learn and need extra time to prepare for their various tasks. Demands multiply as ministerial skills and competency improve. It is easy to get caught up in ministry to others and to neglect our own spiritual growth.

It helps to reflect on Jesus, the active teacher and healer, who struggled to find time for prayer to the One he addressed as Abba. Our spiritual tradition, which often celebrates the monk as the great model of holiness, has not been as attentive to the example of Jesus, who chose an active life in the world rather than the secluded life of a monk. For campus ministers, the path to holiness passes through the world of action. All six ministerial practices have a spiritual dimension. We must develop a situational spirituality in which our ministry prompts brief moments of prayer: for example, success leads to expressions of praise and gratitude; challenges to petitionary prayers; and culpable failures to requests for forgiveness.

Ministerial activities can also lead to other spiritual practices: for instance, preaching demands prayerful reflection on scripture; and teaching calls for the study of theology, which can aid spiritual growth.

Busy campus ministers benefit from a regular spiritual regimen. All Christians need a healthy alternating rhythm between activity and contemplation that fits their personality and circumstances. Campus ministers need a regimen that helps alert us to the presence of Christ in our daily activities and can be done even on hectic days. New campus ministers might want to experiment with various times of the day and with various practices such as centering prayer, *lectio divina*, Liturgy of the Hours, or the Rosary. Those who struggle to find time for a daily spiritual regimen should recall the example of Jesus and the consistent advice of the spiritual masters.

DIALOGUE WITH FRANCIS

Although the pope has not, to my knowledge, explicitly addressed campus ministers, he has offered advice to others (lay leaders, seminarians, priests, and bishops) that can be applied to those who lead the church on campus. Guided by Francis, campus ministers function as servants, always available to the community, helping the members to grow and participate in the mission of the church. Effective leaders know how to position themselves with the people: sometimes in front leading the way; sometimes among the people to learn of their joys and challenges; and many times, behind them to help those who cannot keep up. Servant leaders are close to their people, knowing and loving them as individuals and being available to them day and night, sleeping with the phone close by, as Francis puts it. They engage in "the mysticism of encounter," accepting others in their uniqueness, and listening to them without fear and without vanity that implies superiority. Campus ministers who offer close personal service to students, faculty members, and administrators are like shepherds "living with the smell of the sheep" in the now well-known phrase of Francis. Servant leaders must manifest God's infinite mercy to those on the periphery as well as to those who find a home in the campus faith community. Applying advice that the pope gave to bishops, campus ministers should be servants with a deep prayer life so they can share with their people "the joy and love of God" and "the flame of the Risen Christ." Campus ministers should nourish a deep spiritual life so they can be "sentinels" on campus, always ready "to restore the faith" and "inspire charity," without dozing off into a nostalgic fascination with a past that has already been and gone. The pope not only gives valuable advice, but also provides creative leadership, rooted in the Gospel and responsive to a changing world. Campus ministers who catch his spirit will find ways to create communities of faith that are welcoming and nourishing.

7

PEER MINISTRY

This chapter examines peer ministry as a support system for collegians and reflects on the numerous ways Catholic collegians serve their peers. I have always been impressed with the generosity of students who understand the social dimension of their faith. Peer ministry programs provide them with opportunities to serve others and support the church on campus. The following originally appeared in an edited book on secular support systems for collegians.[1] Hopefully, it will help campus ministers improve their peer ministry programs.

PEER MINISTRY:
LEADERSHIP AND SERVICE ON CAMPUS

Ten collegians are gathered to make final plans for a weekend retreat they are conducting for other undergraduate students. They have been meeting regularly for many weeks, praying together, determining the theme of the retreat, assembling ideas for their individual presentations, and working out the housing, food, and transportation details. In the process, the planners have learned a great deal about their faith and have deepened their religious commitments. They've had fun together while gradually achieving a sense of group solidarity. Their goal is to provide a prayerful, growth-producing experience for the students making the retreat. Recalling when another team of student leaders provided them with an enjoyable weekend of prayer, witness presentation, and informal discussions, they are determined to offer similar positive experiences for other students.

111

These ten collegians are involved in the rapidly growing church activity commonly known as "peer ministry." Ministry, in general, is currently a topic of great interest within my own Catholic community. The respected Catholic theologian Thomas O'Meara, for instance, defines Christian ministry as "the public activity of a baptized follower of Jesus Christ, following from the Spirit's charism and an individual personality on behalf of a Christian community to witness to, serve, and realize the kingdom of God."[2] This definition suggests that ministry involves service to others that is performed publicly and has some official character. At the same time, it recognizes that individuals have unique personalities enhanced by free gifts and talents that are to be utilized not merely for self-fulfillment but for the common good. Moreover, the definition implicitly assumes some sort of training or preparation for ministry, so that it is performed not only with conviction, but with intelligence. The goal of this activity is to help humanize the world by fostering a community of justice, love, and peace.

The word "peer" indicates that this purposeful service is carried out by individuals interacting with others who are in similar circumstances or have had similar experiences. We are familiar with reforming alcoholics assisting one another and with support groups of divorced people helping each other adjust to new lifestyles. In our context, peer ministry refers to the activity of collegians who, energized by commitment to their religious tradition and enlightened by some training, reach out to serve the needs of their fellow students.

PEER MINISTRY AS COMMUNITY BUILDING

In the 1970s, Lutheran campus ministers at the University of Cincinnati developed a student outreach program that doubled the size of their worshiping community in one year, dramatically improving the quality of their community life. This program grew out of the realization that two-thirds of their Lutheran students were from outside the city and lived on campus or in nearby apartments. These students, living in a large urban university of almost 40,000 students, felt strong needs for a sense of identity and community. In response, the campus ministers trained twenty-five students each year to take responsibility for befriending four to six incoming Lutheran freshmen. The training, which included prayer and imaginative teaching techniques, taught the peer ministers to show personal concern for the other students. Their task was to contact the incoming freshmen the first week of school, invite them to the weekly worship service, as well as other activities, and to stay in contact with them throughout the academic year. Many friendships developed from these contacts, helping to spread greater care and concern throughout the Lutheran community on campus. Students in the program learned through experience to adopt a casual approach rather than to put pressure on the freshmen. Staff members met periodically with a few of the peer ministers, guiding and encouraging them so that they would continue to meet their responsibilities. This program is a fine example of the kind of community building that students with proper training and motivation can promote.

There are, of course, diverse ways of accomplishing this goal. On some campuses, for example, students develop a sense of community around Bible study and shared prayer. At large residential schools served by a sacramental ministry, Catholic students participate in the Rite of Christian Initiation of Adults (RCIA), a year-long program of preparing individuals to join the church. Peer ministers connect interested students, serve as their sponsors or spiritual companions throughout the preparation period, and participate in the initiation rites during the Easter season.

Many campus ministers make community building their top priority, since a vibrant community of faith is the basis for many other ministerial functions. Those who invite students to share in this task usually find dedicated individuals willing to reach out to their peers.

Peer ministers are often effective because they have experienced both the isolation and loneliness of campus life and the positive rewards of involvement in a community of faith. Thus, they can speak about their experiences in a way their peers can understand and appreciate. Ideally, their training would include communication skills, with a strong emphasis on listening as well as a knowledge of the main teachings of the religious community they represent. Peer ministers often become better community members precisely because of the service they perform. They feel more responsible for the community and become more aware of its positive potential to provide roots, identity, and opportunities for service.

However, there is also a danger. Peer ministers may be tempted to think that because church involvement has enriched their lives, they should aggressively recruit others even if it means using pressure tactics and inducing guilt feelings. Campuses today are filled with aggressive religious proselytizers who passionately desire to save others from sin and bring them into the circle of light. Christians who believe they have a pipeline to God and a monopoly on the truth not only turn off open-minded people but threaten to put the whole ministry of community building in a bad light. This is a good reason for providing peer ministers with proper supervision and periodic evaluations. Such oversight will, no doubt, uncover some neglect of duty, but more importantly, it will help prevent ministers from employing militant tactics that give religion a bad name.

Catholic theology insists that the task of community building flows from the ecclesial nature of Christianity as well as from the interdependent character of human existence. The general perception of the divine-human relationship was exemplified in the life of Jesus Christ who, led by the Spirit, gathered a community of followers. Through parables and awesome signs, he proclaimed a community of love in which all human beings were to live in peace and harmony. His death and resurrection, far from destroying the community of his disciples, brought a renewed sense of solidarity and mission. Throughout Christian history, all baptized persons have been called to take responsibility for forming the church into a genuine community of worship and service.

Catholic peer ministers should have an understanding of an authentic religious community and its theological background. They are not simply recruiting for a campus organization such as a fraternity or sorority. They are calling people together around transcendent values and the deepest beliefs. Motivation for their ministry is derived from their conviction that it is a response to the call of God, who wills the solidarity of the whole human family. They need not be pushy because they realize that salvation is finally the work of God, who is merciful toward all people. This theology should remind them that the quality of life in the faith community is a more important consideration than increasing the numbers. Their real task is to help make the faith community into what it claims to be: a sign and instrument of the final union of all people in God's family.

PEER MINISTRY AS LITURGICAL PARTICIPATION

When I served as campus minister at Bowling Green State University in Ohio, we had a group of about thirty singers and musicians who provided the music for our weekend Masses. A few were music majors, but most were not. All were willing to share their musical talents with the university parish. They practiced twice a week. The student leader was an excellent guitarist who sometimes composed his own music. At this large residential state university, there were five Masses every weekend to accommodate over two thousand students and faculty who attended. Some of the musicians came only to one Mass, but a core group was usually present at all five. They had been schooled in a long tradition that music at Mass was not a performance but an integral part of the worship. Because of their reverent and prayerful attitude, they could enhance the participation of the whole congregation. On Sundays after the 11:00 a.m. Mass, they ate together, relaxed, and socialized. Many close friendships were formed in the group that eventually led to a few solid marriages. Some of the members gathered regularly to read the Scriptures and pray. Many of them also performed other ministerial functions within the university parish. The core group was asked by the university to stage a program for incoming freshmen each year. This proved to be an important and enjoyable extension of their ministry.

The dedication and good example of these young people often inspired me. I can recall weekends, for instance, when their great enthusiasm energized me for presiding at the Masses, even though I was tired and preoccupied. Students frequently reported that the marvelous music at Mass not only helped draw them to church but also enabled them to achieve a more prayerful spirit. Thus, these dedicated musicians exercised an important peer ministry by sharing their talents and gifts to enhance the worship of the whole congregation.

Around the country, Catholic students are heavily involved in various liturgical ministries. Individuals help plan for the Masses, provide hospitality by serving as ushers, and proclaim the Word. Artists, dancers, and other creative people contribute their talents to produce imaginative and aesthetically pleasing liturgies. Some are specially chosen by the leaders of the church to distribute communion at Mass. This is usually seen as a privilege extended to individual students because they are serious about the Christian life and have contributed to the well-being of the church. The Catholic liturgical renewal has taken hold among collegians. Residential campuses across the country report well-attended, vibrant liturgies. Visitors to campus are often impressed with the participation and prayerfulness of the students. There is no doubt that committed peer ministers have played a key role in this remarkable liturgical revival.

Recruiting liturgical ministers is easier if there is a tradition of well-planned Masses that respond to the needs of collegians. Campus ministers have the responsibility of teaching students that they are co-responsible for enhancing the quality of the community worship. If collegians feel that the Mass is truly their communal prayer and not merely the priest's task, they are more likely to volunteer their time and talents. Adequate training gives them motivation to sustain the effort. I know of a university parish, for example, that provides excellent training for those who proclaim the Scripture at Mass. A strong tradition of skilled reading attracts quality students to that ministry. They are carefully trained in oral communication as well as modern biblical interpretation. They are encouraged to write their own short commentaries, which they read to the congregation before proclaiming the Scripture passages. After the Masses, one of the staff members offers them a brief critique of their reading. A couple of times during the year all the readers gather for a short retreat, which reminds them of the spiritual dimension of their ministry.

PEER MINISTRY AS FORMATION

Each year at our university parish, one recent graduate is invited to join our staff for a year of volunteer service. Our volunteers make a substantial sacrifice of time and money since they delay entry into graduate school or the job market by a year. We pay them a $1,200 stipend for the year plus car allowance and medical insurance. Adult members of the parish are encouraged to help defray these expenses by sponsoring the volunteer. We have been blessed with outstanding young people who have contributed their unique talents to the life of the parish as well as helping with some of the routine tasks.

A few years ago, our volunteer, Kevin, was especially involved in the kind of teaching and learning that we associate with the "ministry of formation." Ministers dedicated to formation must strive for an adult appropriation of their faith so that they can enable others to grow in their knowledge and appreciation of Christ. As part of his own formation during his year of service, Kevin did a "great books" course. Under my direction, he read twelve classic works, including Plato's *Republic*, Aristotle's *Ethics*, Augustine's *Confessions*, Kierkegaard's *Fear and*

Trembling, and Heidegger's *Introduction to Metaphysics,* relating major ideas of each to the theology of the great German Jesuit, Karl Rahner, as represented in his masterwork, *Foundations of Christian Faith.* We met regularly to discuss each of the authors, emphasizing the historical context of their thought as well as the current relevance of their insights. His final paper summarizing his understanding of these authors enabled him to achieve a more refined philosophical and theological synthesis.

Based on his own program of personal formation, Kevin was able to share his faith with others in a variety of ways. He team-taught a course on Christian attitudes toward human sexuality. His peer ministry of formation extended to organizing about twenty collegians in a project of making pizzas to be given to the poor at a local food distribution center. His appropriation of the philosophical and theological tradition enabled him to make valuable contributions to our weekly planning for upcoming Masses. He incorporated a spiritual dimension into the guitar lessons he offered to other students. His studies led naturally to twelve appearances on my radio program, in which we discussed the contemporary significance of the authors he read.

Additionally, his volunteer experience has further enriched his doctoral studies in psychology. His "great books" course has given him a broad context for his specialized studies. Only a few graduates are willing to give a year of service, although one campus ministry program at a large university recently had four fine applicants for their volunteer position.

More typically, the ministry of formation is carried out by students on a limited part-time basis. They, for instance, plan and execute retreats for their peers. The planning often motivates the leaders to deepen their own faith while the retreat setting provides opportunities for speaking openly about their beliefs and values. Collegians also run Bible study classes using packaged programs produced by experts. In addition to such programs, the students share their faith informally while talking with their peers about deep feelings and the struggles of life.

We suffer from a general lack of religious literacy in our society, and the current collegians are no exception. This lack of religious knowledge hampers the ministry of formation carried out by students. Individuals cannot pass on or share what they do not have. Unfortunately, campus ministers have not had enormous success in recruiting students for theology classes or scripture courses that employ the modern historical critical methods.

Nevertheless, we must insist on training programs for peer ministers with a strong theological orientation in which students can learn the fundamentals of their faith. Reflection on ministerial practices is an effective way of gaining this knowledge. Campus ministers, for example, can gather students who have run a retreat and lead them in a Scriptural reflection on the deeper meaning of their experience. Students who expect to help form others must be in a process of formation themselves. If they expect to witness to their faith in effective ways after they leave school, they will have to achieve an adult appropriation of the faith. Individuals with a high school understanding of their faith and advanced specialized knowledge in other fields are in danger of living a dualistic life or of giving up their faith. Students generally are looking for an authentic integrated way of living humanly. An effective ministry of formation must respond to this need.

In the nineteenth century, Blessed John Henry Cardinal Newman, a convert to Catholicism and the patron of Catholic campus ministers in the United States, argued that religious knowledge was essential to the well-educated person. He reminds us that religious knowledge has an inherent value, constitutes a legitimate academic discipline, and is part of our cultural heritage. It can broaden our tolerance of other's values and serve as an integrating principle for the rest of learning. Students have a right to know about religion because this knowledge is essential for understanding themselves and their world.

There are now indications that this insight is gradually being recognized. Students frequently express anger or dismay over their meager religious education. At some universities, religious studies courses are crowded with eager students. Small groups of students are seeking contemporary scripture studies. If these trends are fostered, we will see an increase in effective peer ministers devoted to helping form others in the path.

PEER MINISTRY AS SERVICE TO THE ACADEMIC WORLD

Brandt, a senior at the University of Toledo, was heavily involved in campus activities ever since his freshman year. During his junior year, he was elected student government president and carried out his duties with tremendous dedication and energy. Brandt's approach included staying in close contact with his fellow students, arranging opportunities for them to express their views, and serving on numerous university committees, including the very influential budget committee. Many administrators and faculty members came to respect his commitment as well as his expertise. The new president of the university, for example, made use of his broad knowledge of student needs and interests. Brandt used his term in office to make valuable contributions to the well-being of the university.

During the past two years, we have met regularly as part of a one-to-one faculty-student dialogue program. Over lunch, we discuss a wide range of issues, including ways of improving campus life. For me the conversations are stimulating and informative. It is marvelous to encounter a student who combines a passionate desire to humanize the university with a developing political sense of how to accomplish this endeavor. My contribution to the ongoing conversation includes perspectives and insights derived from many years of experience as a campus minister. In my interactions with Brandt, I have played the roles of spiritual guide, theological consultant, academic advisor, and friendly critic. Part of my function has been to provide a link with his Catholic heritage. During his year as student government president, Brandt attended our Masses regularly but was not involved in other aspects of our parish life. That arrangement seemed fitting, and I made no effort to prompt greater parish involvement on his part. My hope was that our common religious heritage as reflected in the life of our parish would be a source of strength and guidance for him as he carried out his valuable duties in the academic community. Because of the nature and depth of Brandt's commitments, I considered his campus activities to be a very important type of peer ministry—a ministry of service to the academic world.

From my experience, many Catholic students do not immediately make explicit connections between such activities and their faith. Nevertheless, the connections exist and should be made explicit.

The church offers these students a spiritual home that provides nourishment and wisdom to strengthen and guide their efforts. Collegians need help to integrate their religious heritage with their involvement in the world. Campus ministers can facilitate this process by bringing together students involved in campus life to reflect on their experiences in the light of their religious tradition. Students who go through this process will be better prepared to contribute to the common good throughout their lives.

While these reflections on peer ministry are rooted in the particularities of my Catholic tradition, they are in no way meant to be exclusive. My hope, rather, is that they will reveal more universal perspectives and general insights that will facilitate the continuing development of peer ministry in all religious traditions.

DIALOGUE WITH FRANCIS

In a June 7, 2013, talk to students attending Jesuit schools, Pope Francis highlighted the virtue of magnanimity, which inclines us to hold noble ideals and to strive to do wonderful things in response to "what God asks of us." Magnanimity, which expands our mental and emotional horizons, enables us to do the little routine things of everyday life with "a great heart open to God and to others."

Francis went on to reflect on "two fundamental values" important to students: freedom and service. Freedom is not simply doing whatever we like or seeing how far we can go. It is, rather, the ability to assess what promotes and what retards our authentic development and to "opt for the good." The pope exhorts students: "Be free for goodness," have courage to "go against the tide," develop "a backbone" so you can face the demands of life. The pope encourages students to take part in activities that thrust them out of "their own small world" and immerse them in the larger world of others, including those in need. Francis encourages students to be "true champions" serving others. To develop the virtue of magnanimity with inner freedom and a spirit of service, students need spiritual formation. They must learn to listen to Christ, their companion and friend, who speaks to us through prayer, the Bible, and the events of daily life. Christ is our guide to a happy and fulfilling life, doing great things for God.

Inspired by Francis, campus ministers challenge collegians to live up to their highest ideals. They encourage students to use their talents and gifts to build the faith community and to serve as ambassadors for Christ on campus. They establish peer ministry programs and provide training for student participants. This entire effort has a positive tone and message for students: you have specific gifts that can enrich the church; you can make a difference on campus; you can help students in need; you can enhance the ministry of the leaders. This message can be communicated in several ways: homilies that highlight the virtue of magnanimity; counseling that helps students discern their distinctive gifts; celebrations that recognize the contributions of student leaders; and liturgies that include a blessing for peer ministers.

Peer ministers can be especially effective in the residence halls, running small-group programs: for example, a weekly gathering to reflect on the Sunday readings; periodic discussions of common concerns such as forming healthy relationships; praise and worship sessions that include familiar music and shared prayer. Student leaders need training to run effective small groups and resource materials that fit their needs and reflect the best of the Catholic tradition. Campus ministers have already developed excellent residence hall programs around the country that can serve as models for those looking to start and improve similar activities. Pope Francis, with his emphasis on magnanimity, is a great ally in the effort to expand and improve programming in residence halls and in the important task of getting more students involved in various forms of peer ministry.

IV

FORMING
THE
FAITH
COMMUNITY

8

AN EXPERIENCE OF COMMUNITY

In treating the six ministerial functions, *Empowered by the Spirit* begins with Forming Community. Noting both the positive experience of community on campus as well as the alienation and isolation felt by some, the pastoral letter notes that the call to form communities of faith flows from the example and teachings of Jesus, who gathered and instructed a community of followers. To guide the community-building efforts of the church on campus, the pastoral presents an extended description of an ideal community of faith:

> The Mystery that rules over our lives is named and worshipped. Dedication to Christ is fostered, and openness to all truth, goodness, and beauty is maintained. The life of the Spirit is nourished and discussed. Positive images of God, Christ, Mary, and the afterlife warm the heart and structure the imagination. The common good is emphasized and personal development encouraged. Individuals experience true freedom and at the same time accept responsibility for the well-being of the group. Traditional wisdom is available and the best contemporary insights are valued. Prayerful liturgies enable us to praise God with full hearts and create a sense of belonging, as well as nourish people for a life of service. Members are known by name and newcomers are welcomed. Unity of faith is celebrated while legitimate pluralism is recognized. Individuals find both support and challenge and can share their joys and sorrows. The members hunger for justice and have the courage to fight the

dehumanizing tendencies in the culture. The community knows the sorrows of life but remain a people of hope. In this ideal community of faith, the members are of one heart and mind (Acts 4:32) and receive the spirit of wisdom which brings them to full knowledge of Jesus Christ who is the head of the Church (Eph 1:17–23).[1]

Effective campus ministry programs use a variety of means to establish vibrant communities of faith: weekend liturgies with upbeat music and relevant homilies; the adult catechumenate process that engages the whole community; prayer groups that encourage mutual sharing; and service programs that unite participants in helping people in need. The pastoral letter concludes its treatment of forming community: "This crucial aspect of campus ministry is worthy of vigorous and creative efforts so that the Catholic community can be an authentic sign and instrument of the kingdom on campus" (n. 44).

What follows are some viable suggestions that campus ministers can use to form communities of faith. This section also highlights the way effective campus ministry programs enrich the whole church.

STUDENT LEADERS ON COMMUNITY BUILDING

In 1986, almost five hundred collegians from forty-six states gathered in the New Orleans area during their Christmas break for the second annual conference of the reconstituted National Catholic Student Coalition. The prayer service at the beginning of the first working day symbolized the vitality, creativity, and sense of community that characterize many collegians today. The service was carefully planned by one of the regional groupings of the Coalition and included a grand entrance with large banners, a tasteful liturgical dance, a reverent proclamation of the Word, and a prayerful recital of the Lord's Prayer. A judicious use of bells, candles, and incense enhanced the ceremony, linking us with a larger tradition. The atmosphere was informal, the dress was casual, and the reactions were spontaneous. Students from all over the country were obviously at home with this style of prayer. Through the prayer, they possibly recognized familiar elements from the worship on their own campuses. The good feelings generated by the prayer service resonated with their experiences of genuine Christian community.

These students have come to appreciate that prayer can break down barriers and draw people together.

My goal in presenting at this conference was to build on this positive experience and indicate the major ideas outlined in the recently completed pastoral letter, *Empowered by the Spirit*. Having worked with the editorial committee on this pastoral for almost three years, I was anxious to test its usefulness with this group of student leaders. Through extensive consultations with administrators, faculty, students, and campus ministers, it became clear that the formation of vibrant faith communities is a high ministerial priority on campuses around the country. Thus, the pastoral letter, after locating campus ministry in the context of the general relationship between the church and higher education, discusses the formation of Christian community as the first of various ministerial activities performed by the church on campus.

In fact, a significant effort already goes into the formation and enrichment of Catholic communities on campus. Despite the problems created by a transient population, considerable progress has been made. On many residential campuses, vibrant celebrations of the Eucharist are the center of the community life. As a result, we have produced large numbers of college graduates who have positive experiences of the community-building power of the liturgy. They are an extremely valuable resource for the whole church and we need to find better ways of tapping this potential. On commuter campuses, community building is more difficult, but even in this situation creative campus ministers accomplish a great deal through such activities as Bible study, group prayer, and retreats. Active faith communities provide a home for students who must cope with many alienating forces on campus, and offer a setting in which individuals can contribute their gifts and talents to the common good.

In my presentation, I described a former student who came to a large state university from a very familiar and comfortable Catholic background. Amid his initial anxiety, he found the university parish, met some friends, got involved in the parish, and contributed his leadership skills to its well-being. He made the church on campus his primary community, which served as a support system and provided opportunities for his personal development. After graduation, he married a young woman he met in the Newman Club. They settled down in a small town and became active in the local Catholic parish, serving on the liturgy committee, which they helped energize.

This young couple is typical of many Catholic collegians who have enjoyed a positive relationship with the faith community on campus and are exemplary in their determination to translate their collegiate experience into another parish setting.

As leaders, I noted, they need to draw on the wisdom of the Christian tradition in their efforts to make their faith communities more welcoming and effective. We reflected on the significance of Jesus from various perspectives: the community builder, who chose the Twelve as a symbol of his intent to form the new people of God; the miracle worker, who through his healings brought outcasts into the community; the friend of those on the margins, who broke down cultural barriers and called all into a richer unity.

Thus, we are reminded that leaders in the church are not to throw their weight around, but are to be servants who reconcile diverse groupings and are attentive to the alienated and the lonely. The faith community is not merely another social group, such as a sorority or a ski club. It is based on commitment to Christ and shared gospel values. The members are co-responsible for the community and are empowered by the Spirit to help humanize the world. The church on campus is not an isolated enclave where collegians can do their own thing for four years; it is an organic part of a larger church that mediates a rich tradition and invites a lifelong commitment to service. Extensive active involvement in the faith community itself is not possible, nor desirable, for all collegians. Leaders should recognize this and not make excessive demands. At the same time, they should encourage involvement in other campus activities and promote efforts to spread the kingdom in the world. The good feelings generated at the morning prayer service remind us that genuine community building takes intelligent effort and can lead to generous service that fosters the liberation of all.

Based on these introductory remarks, the students engaged in animated small-group discussions on how they could improve the faith communities on their own campuses and translate their idealism into practical strategies for overcoming apathy and alienation. A bishop who was an observer at the conference told me that these young people were indeed a sign of hope. Observing their enthusiasm and feeling their spirit, I recognized more deeply both the truth and significance of his comment.

An Experience of Community

DIALOGUE WITH FRANCIS

For Pope Francis, the family is the prime experiential model for healthy community life. In the family setting, we learn to receive and give love, to live together in harmony, and to help one another grow. Family bonds provide the foundation for the stability of society, for the work of education, and for "integral human development." In the family, "the essential cell of society and the church,"[2] we become aware of our own worth and the dignity of every single person, so that we can treat each other as "a true sister or brother."

God's plan is to make all people members of "a single family," enjoying the warmth of divine love. The church is "rooted in the great plan" to call all people into the divine life of sons and daughters. The image of the church as the Body of Christ extols "the vital union of Christ with believers and of believers among themselves." Christian faith is not simply a private decision of an individual but, by its very nature, is open to the We of the church. As happens in healthy families, so individuals in the community of faith can grow to maturity and learn a fundamental respect for others. Francis put the family in the center of his agenda to renew the church by holding the Extraordinary General Assembly of the Synod of Bishops in 2014, followed by the Ordinary General Assembly in October 2015, with the theme of the vocation and mission of the family in the church and in the contemporary world. He delighted in the strong disagreements and passionate debates among the synod fathers, the kind of dynamic interactions we might find in a healthy family.

In response, Pope Francis issued his apostolic exhortation on family life entitled *Amoris Laetitia* (*The Joy of Love*). The long document (over 50,000 words with 391 footnotes, organized in nine chapters), dated on the feast of St. Joseph, March 19, 2016, has generated significant reaction in church circles and in the secular media, much of it focused on controversial issues, especially communion for divorced and remarried Catholics. Most of the exhortation, however, deals with broader issues, such as the biblical understanding of marriage, the contemporary challenges to family life, church teaching on marriage, the procreation and education of children, and a family-oriented spirituality. Of special interest is chapter 4, "Love in Marriage." The eminent theologian, Richard Gaillardetz, a married father of four boys, sees this "extraordinary chapter" as a "remarkable example of pastoral encouragement" and as "an inspirational meditation" that "could be put into the hands of engaged and married couples," confident that "they might read it, understand it, and profit by it."

The chapter begins with an extended reflection on Paul's popular Hymn to Love (1 Cor 13:1–7), which includes insightful commentaries on each of the noted characteristics of love: patient, kind, not jealous or boastful, not arrogant or rude, not irritable or resentful, rejoicing in right not wrong, and, finally, bearing, believing, hoping, and enduring all things. In discussing the first characteristic, for example, Francis points out that the Greek word translated as "patient" is used in the Greek version of the Hebrew Scriptures to speak about our God who is "slow to anger" and always merciful to sinners.

Being patient does not mean allowing ourselves to be used or mistreated, but it does suggest that we exercise restraint by not acting on impulses that could give offense to others. We run into trouble when we think family life should be perfect and expect everything to go our way. Then anything that is out of order in ordinary family life can make us impatient and prone to angry responses. When we are unable "to control our impulses," we risk turning our families into "battlegrounds." With great pastoral wisdom, Francis insists that the key to avoiding impatience, which causes family strife, is accepting others in their uniqueness. In other words: "Patience takes root when I recognize that other people also have a right to live in this world, just as they are" (n. 92). Genuine love accepts others even when they are imperfect and behave in ways we do not like. This fundamental acceptance enables us to stay patient with others even when they unsettle our plans or get in our way. True Christian love exercises patience even amid the stresses of contemporary family life.

The apostolic exhortation offers valuable interpretations and applications of all the Pauline characteristics of love, including the last one: love endures all things. Again, drawing on the meaning of the Greek term, Francis insists that "love bears every trial with a positive attitude," standing "firm in hostile surroundings." Genuine endurance not only tolerates aggravations; it is constantly ready to confront any challenge. In the second chapter, Francis noted some of those challenges, including: lack of housing, pornography, abuse of minors, legal dismantling of the family, violence against women, rampant individualism, and fear of entrapment. Love "never gives up, even in the darkest hour," but demonstrates a "dogged heroism" and an "irrepressible commit-ment to goodness." To exemplify his point, Francis raises up Martin Luther King Jr., who "met every kind of trial and tribulation with frater-nal love." He goes on to cite at length one of King's sermons, in which he insisted we overcome hate with enduring love by seeing "the image of God" in other people, even those who seek to hurt us. When we "rise to the level of love," we do not try to defeat enemies but concentrate on defeating systems that breed hatred. We need dedicated persons who "inject within the very structure of the universe that strong and power-ful element of love" (n. 118).[3]

Francis applies Dr. King's insight to family life. Christian love practiced in families "never gives up," not yielding to "resentment, scorn for others or the desire to hurt or to gain some advantage." The pope then interjects a personal note, as he sometimes does throughout the long exhortation, expressing his amazement at divorced spouses, who later come to the aid of their former married partners when they encounter some illness or other suffering. For Francis, this exemplifies a love that never gives up and endures all things.

Many couples pick Paul's "Hymn to Love" as one of the read-ings for their wedding ceremony. Spending some time with the pope's commentary will enrich their preparation for marriage. We might also anticipate fresh approaches to preaching on this hymn as priests and deacons gradually appropriate some of the valuable insights found in this opening of the fourth chapter of the encyclical.

The next section of the chapter is headed "Growing in Conjugal Love." Francis says the love between husband and wife is enriched by the grace of the sacrament of marriage that combines "the warmth of friendship and erotic passion" in an "effective union" that "endures long after emotions and passion subside." This powerful love "reflects the unbroken covenant between Christ and humanity," a broad con-cept that moves beyond the usual Christ and the church image. Mar-riage is "the icon" of God's love for us, which makes "the two spouses one single existence" (n. 121).

Francis follows this lofty description of marriage with a crucial caution: "There is no need to lay upon two limited persons the tre-mendous burden of having to reproduce perfectly the union existing between Christ and his Church." Accepting this realistic limitation frees couples to engage in a "dynamic process" that gradually brings them closer to the ideal. The pope makes another important move by adopting the teaching of St. Thomas Aquinas that, after the love that unites us to God, conjugal love is "the greatest form of friendship," which means married couples are called "to share and shape together the whole of life" in an "indissoluble exclusivity," characterized by "reciprocity, intimacy, warmth, stability and the resemblance born of a shared life" (n. 123).

Statistical studies support linking conjugal love with friendship. Married couples who consider their spouse as their best friend have a better chance of sustaining their commitment and making a happy marriage. Christian couples who see marriage as a "covenant before God" and their love as part of the divine plan have added motivation for staying together in a permanent and definitive union.

Drawing on the teachings of Vatican II, Francis presents marriage as "a friendship marked by passion," which promotes "an ever more stable and intense union." The Council taught that "marriage was not instituted solely for the procreation of children" but also that mutual love might "grow and mature" and "be properly expressed" (GS 50). Conjugal love "leads the partners to a free and mutual self-giving, experienced in tenderness and action, and permeating their entire lives" (n. 125).

After analyzing human emotions in general, which are not in themselves morally good or evil, Francis presents sexuality as "a marvelous gift" from God, which must be cultivated and directed to preserve it as "an authentic value." Relying on previous teaching of Pope John Paul II, Francis insists that sexuality is not a means of gratification or entertainment; it is "an interpersonal language," which takes seriously the "sacred and inviolable dignity" of the partner. The erotic dimension of love is not simply "a permissible evil"; it is a "gift from God that enriches the relationship of the spouses" and reveals "the marvels of which the human heart is capable" (n. 150–52).

Having established a positive Christian outlook on sexuality, Francis offers a realistic assessment of how sex can be depersonalized as an instrument of "self-assertion" and "selfish satisfaction," in treating the body of another as an object of pleasure to be used and discarded at will. In marriage, sex can be used to manipulate and control one's spouse, violating the essential notion of marriage as an interpersonal communion based on equality and respect. As the pope puts it: "Sexuality is inseparably at the service" of "conjugal friendship" that seeks the good of the spouse (n. 156).

Some married Catholic theologians, along with others, have criticized Pope John Paul II's theology of the body for overly romanticizing the total self-giving involved in marital intercourse. They can find greater realism in the statement of Francis: "The ideal of marriage cannot be seen purely as generous donation and self-sacrifice, where each spouse renounces all personal needs and seeks only the other's good without concern for personal satisfaction" (n. 157). Spouses need to accept their "own vulnerabilities and needs" and to welcome various expressions of love from their partners. Those who want to give love must be ready to receive love as a gift.

Francis continues his realistic examination of conjugal love by pointing out that with today's longer life spans, couples must maintain their commitment for many decades, during which physical appearances change and sexual desire may diminish. The pope reminds couples that they are companions on life's journey and that they love their spouse for "who they are, not simply for their body" (n. 164). He encourages couples to renew their initial commitment frequently and to come up with "a shared and lasting life project." He advises believers to pray to the Holy Spirit for strength "to confirm, direct and transform" their lives as they face each new stage of their shared journey.

According to Francis, "Dialogue is essential for experiencing, expressing and fostering love in marriages and family life," but this requires a "long and demanding apprenticeship" since men and women, young and old, communicate in such diverse ways. The pope offers some helpful suggestions for improving family dialogue. Listen carefully to the other person. Be sure we have heard them out before offering an opinion or advice. Cultivate "an interior silence" so we can listen without distractions. Put aside our own needs and worries to make space for the needs of others. He also reminds married couples that their spouse often is not looking for a solution to a problem but simply wants to feel that their partner acknowledges their pain, disappointments, fears, and anger as well as their "hopes and dreams." To do this we need "to put ourselves in their shoes and try to peer into their hearts, to perceive their deepest concerns and to take them as a point of departure for further dialogue" (n. 138). We should "keep an open mind," ready to change or expand our own limited ideas and opinions. We need to free ourselves from feeling that we all must be alike. In discussing difficult issues, we should choose our words carefully so as not to offend the other. Avoid venting anger or adopting a patronizing tone. Set aside the need "to win an argument or to be proved right." Resist the temptation to see family members as "rivals," while expressing genuine concern and affection for them. Finally, Francis ends his treatment of dialogue with a reminder to married couples that they will be better dialogue partners if they "have something to say," which is "the fruit of an interior richness nourished by reading, personal reflection, prayer and openness to the world around us" (n. 141).

Pope Francis has produced a marvelous resource for enriching marriages and family life. We hope that his penetrating insights and wise advice will reach a wide audience.

As the pope has noted elsewhere, the family is a privileged place for the experience of beauty, truth, and goodness that opens our hearts to the God of love. With a pastor's realism, he recognizes the dark side of family life, but insists that the light of divine grace is stronger than all the dark forces. When God sent his Son into the world to save the whole human family, the Word took flesh in a specific Jewish family with parents, Mary and Joseph, who were open to God's great gift. Transformed by the presence of Christ, the family becomes a source of hope. Francis raises up grandparents as the "living memory of the family," who keep alive the great traditions the family needs to continue to grow and move forward. Those who watched Francis interact with young people on his visit to the United States know that he has special affection for the next generation, the ones who hold the future, the ones charged to humanize culture and create a more just and peaceful society. Healthy families, places of "divine citizenship," prepare the next generation to live as good citizens of the earthly city that flourishes when grounded on beauty, truth, and goodness.

Guided by Francis, campus ministers can articulate their vision for the faith community in more concrete terms borrowed from family life. They can speak of the campus church as a home away from home, where everyone is welcomed and appreciated for who they are. In this family of faith, we worship our Father in heaven through our brother Christ. We are brothers and sisters, united by the Spirit, who calls us to help create a more family-like atmosphere on campus.

Campus ministry can improve its programming by keeping the family in mind. Outreach to parents is important: for example, alerting them to ways the Catholic community serves their sons and daughters; reaching out to them when they visit campus (for example, at the beginning of the academic year and on Parents' Weekend); praying for them at Mass; offering them a free meal; providing them with brochures about activities of the campus church; giving them the opportunity to contribute to the church; and other creative ways of making them feel part of a community dedicated to serving their adult children. Those counseling collegians need to be alert to challenges generated by flawed parental relationships. Homilies, discussions, and classes can make the church's renewed teaching on the family developed in the Synod more available. Service programs can reach out to immigrant and refugee families as well as those living below the poverty line. Marriage preparation programs should be attentive to the strengths and weaknesses of families of origin. Preparing collegians for the crucial vocation of parenthood should be part of the general effort to prepare leaders for church and society. Not every campus ministry can implement or even consider all these suggestions. Campus ministers influenced by Pope Francis, however, will be attuned to the opportunities and challenges presented by family life as they carry out the crucial task of forming community.

9

NEWMAN CLUBS REVISITED

The first Newman Club in the United States was established in 1893 at the University of Pennsylvania. It was appropriately named after the recently deceased Cardinal John Henry Newman (1801–90), a convert to Catholicism and a respected scholar who helped establish what became University College in Dublin and wrote the classic work, *The Idea of a University*. Largely under lay leadership, the Newman movement gradually spread throughout the country. Many of the American bishops were leery of supporting Newman Clubs because it undercut their position that Catholic collegians should be attending Catholic colleges and not exposing themselves to the serious temptations on secular campuses. In a typical story from the 1940s, influential lay leaders in Toledo, Ohio, had to convince a reluctant Bishop Karl Altar to allow Catholic students to establish a Newman Club at the University of Toledo. Despite episcopal fears, Newman Clubs spread across the country, reaching peak numbers in the 1950s. What follows argues for the importance and positive role of Newman Clubs in the lives of Catholic collegians on secular campuses.[1]

THE CASE FOR NEWMAN CLUBS

As a campus minister I have experienced very diverse approaches to Newman Clubs or Catholic student organizations. In the early 1970s at Bowling Green State University, our campus ministry staff explicitly emphasized that we did not have a Newman Club. We were a university parish, organized around functional interests in the areas of worship, education, and social outreach. We wanted to avoid the mistakes of the 1950s and early 1960s when Newman Clubs tended to isolate students from campus life and create an artificial Catholic enclave. Thus, while our students were encouraged to participate actively in the life of our university parish, they were expected to find their social and recreational life, for the most part, on campus, and to develop their leadership potential in university-sponsored organizations.

On my arrival at the University of Toledo in 1981, it was necessary to have an official Catholic student organization to gain access to university facilities that we needed for Masses, lectures, meetings, and the like. Our initial efforts, led by my fellow co-pastor, Fr. Dan Zak, to reorganize a long-defunct Newman Club, met with a surprisingly enthusiastic response, and the club has now blossomed into one of the largest and most active organizations on campus. It has over one hundred sixty dues-paying members and the general meetings are well attended. Membership is open to students of all religious backgrounds, provided they support the general aims of the organization. There are eleven standing committees and twenty-two leaders, many of whom returned to campus two weeks before classes began this past fall to participate in a weekend leadership training program. The Newman Club promotes the prayer life of our university parish by organizing retreats and special liturgies. Some of the members provide babysitting service during the Sunday Masses and refreshments afterward. The club sponsors educational programs and social justice projects, such as The Fast for World Harvest. The members organize their own social gatherings, such as a welcome-back-to-campus cookout at the beginning of the academic year, and participate in a wide range of campus activities, including the traditional homecoming events. A veteran observer of the campus scene may well experience a sense of déjà vu while considering these developments.

Our students report that the Newman Club offers them a supportive community that provides an opportunity for personal development and a way of relating to a large impersonal university. It is their home away from home where they can be themselves, a place where they belong and feel accepted. One member expressed the feelings of many when she described her fright at facing a new school with 21,000 students and her immense relief when she was met with smiling faces at her first Newman Club meeting. Such a supportive community enables students to develop their leadership skills, meet new people, and discuss questions of values and meaning. Many say that their involvement has given them greater self-confidence and a desire to reach out and help others. Some report a heightened social consciousness and a stronger desire to contribute to the well-being of the university. Most of the members say that their participation in the Newman Club has enriched their collegiate experience.

This portrayal will sound familiar to at least some campus ministers, as it represents important general trends:

1. There is a renewed interest in Catholic student organizations around the country. After the peak years in the 1950s when most campuses had such organizations, the 1960s and 1970s brought a drastic reduction in their numbers. Today interest in official student groups is again on the rise. One estimate is that over 250 campuses in the country have reestablished organizations with officers, committees, and activities with a religious, educational, service, and social orientation. This new trend was signaled by the official reorganization in early 1985 of the National Catholic Student Coalition as the successor to a previous national student organization that died out during the era of the Vietnam War.

2. Student organizations respond to the hunger for community experienced by many collegians as they encounter impersonal and bureaucratic elements on campus. These groups enable them to move beyond a private individualism and to contribute their time and talent to the well-being of the community. In turn, the association provides the opportunity for friendship, intimacy, communication, and fun with others who share a similar value and belief system.

3. Catholic students can establish their distinctive religious identity in these organizations. There is a greater appreciation today that individuals need to be grounded in their religious heritage to participate confidently and intelligently in ecumenical and interfaith dialogue and live constructively in our pluralistic society. In this effort, it is important that we learn from history and not fall into a narrow Catholic exclusivism. Instead, our student organizations should foster

138

the ideal of committed-openness, which suggests that the more collegians know and appreciate their Catholic tradition, the more open they will be to truth, goodness, and beauty wherever it is found in the academic world and beyond.

4. The student groups of the 1980s have done well in promoting positive religious sentiments through such means as retreats and prayer groups, and in maintaining a sense of openness and tolerance. However, they have been less successful in fostering the kind of theological learning that will enable students to achieve an adult appropriation of the faith so that they can give intelligent Christian witness in the world. Clearly, there is a need for more creative and intense efforts to overcome the religious illiteracy that plagues our culture.

The revival of Catholic student organizations is a response to the pluralism and complexity on campus as well as the desire to establish a clearer Catholic identity. Many campus ministers, recalling the narrowness that characterized these groups in the past, are leery of moving in this direction. However, my experience suggests that these associations can promote the more comprehensive goals of contemporary campus ministry programs without repeating the mistakes of the past.

DIALOGUE WITH FRANCIS

Pope Francis emphasizes pastoral adaptation, insisting that the church must develop creative responses to a rapidly changing world. He points out that young people today face complex situations quite different from previous generations. In his papal ministry, he has not hesitated to make some important organizational changes, such as appointing a cabinet of eight cardinals from around the world to help in the governance of the church.

The pope's example encourages campus ministers to continue improving their ministry to students. In 2003, the staff of Corpus Christi University Parish serving the University of Toledo engaged a public relations firm to help improve their outreach to students. Based on their use of focus groups, our consultants made some very helpful recommendations that we implemented. For example, they suggested that since students make decisions in their first couple of weeks on campus that affect their entire collegiate career, we should make maximum effort to get the Catholic freshmen involved in the parish and our Newman Club during that time. Following this advice, we offer free meals at the parish center; organize social events; give away free t-shirts and mugs with our logo and Mass schedule; plan especially lively liturgies; and provide other activities to attract their attention, get their names, and bring them to our center. The consultants also suggested changing the name of our very successful and highly respected student organization from Newman Club to Catholic Student Association. They pointed out that recognition of the name "Newman" had gone down over the years with fewer parents telling their kids bound for college to join the Newman Club. The word *Catholic* was more likely to attract the students' attention and get them involved in our parish. After much discussion, the current student leaders voted to make the name change, which has worked well, but which initially upset a number of Catholic graduates who treasured their association with the Newman Club and wanted to keep the name. We learned that pastoral adaptation works best when it is respectful of tradition and involves wide consultation. Today more campus ministry programs around the country are using the word *Catholic* to identify themselves. Listening to Pope Francis, campus ministry will be in the forefront of creative pastoral adaptation as it seeks to serve the changing needs of each new generation of students.

In his thought-provoking address celebrating the fiftieth anniversary of the establishment of the Synod of Bishops by Pope Paul VI in 1965, Pope Francis developed the theme of the synodal church. Early in his ministry as Bishop of Rome, he enhanced the synod, "one of the most precious legacies of the Second Vatican Council," by calling the Synod on the Family, which met in 2014 and 2015. His decision was prompted by the conviction that "the way of synodality" is the pathway "God expects from the church of the third millennium."[2]

He grounds his treatment of the synodal church in the Vatican II teaching that the whole people of God, anointed by the Spirit, have a "supernatural sense of faith" and "cannot err in matters of belief." This means that every baptized Christian is "an active subject of evangelization" and should never be reduced to merely a recipient of the gospel message. The people of God have a sense of the faith, "an instinct" to discern the ways the Lord is leading the church.

According to Francis, this teaching of Vatican II guided him to call for wide consultation in preparation for the "two-phased" synod on the family. Furthermore, he realized that "engaging families, listening to their joys and their hopes, their sorrows and their anguish" was necessary for a fruitful discussion among the bishops.[3]

For Francis, "A synodal church is a listening church," which he describes as "a mutual listening in which everyone has something to learn." All the members listen to the Spirit of Truth, preparing them to listen to one another. The synod process, guided by the Holy Spirit, was an experience in listening that involved the faithful, priests, bishops, and the Bishop of Rome, who is the "visible source and foundation" of the unity of the church. Vatican II described the church as a "hierarchical communion" in which the bishops are united with the pope (*cum Petro*) and at the same time are subjected to him as the head of the college of bishops (*sub Petro*). Francis insisted that this structure does not restrict freedom, but guarantees unity. "Synodality...gives us the more appropriate framework to understand the hierarchical ministry,"[4] which is to serve the people of God. For Francis, the church is like "an inverted pyramid," in which the summit is below the base, suggesting that bishops are "the least of all in serving their people and the pope is the "servant of the servants of God." A synodal church always remembers the admonition of Jesus that the leaders in the church must not lord it over others but must be their servant (Matt 20:25–27).

Convinced that we can all learn from the Synod of Bishops, the pope insists that it is "only the most obvious manifestation of a dynamism of communion that inspires all ecclesial decisions."[5] This applies to all church structures, including pastoral councils and episcopal conferences. Speaking personally, Francis said it's clear that "a healthy decentralization is needed,"[6] emphasizing that he does not want to replace local bishops in dealing with all the problems in their territories.

Our common commitment to build a synodal church "is loaded with ecumenical implications," as Francis put it, especially with the Eastern Orthodox Churches. Synodality makes it clear that the pope is not above the church, but inside it, a Bishop among Bishops, leading the Church of Rome, which "presides in charity over all the churches." Francis made his own the recognition of Pope John Paul II of his responsibility "to find a form of exercise of the primary which, while in no way renouncing what is essential to its mission, is nonetheless open to a new situation."[7]

At the end of his address, Francis turned his gaze outward to the human family, declaring that "a synodal church is like a banner lifted up among the nations," which will challenge the exercise of authority by restricted groups of the powerful with "greedy hands." It will also promote the use of authority, founded on "justice and fraternity," that generates "a more beautiful and worthy world for mankind and for the generations that will come after us."[8]

Francis saw this vision of a synodal church at work in both sessions of the Synod on the Family. He was pleased with the open discussion, the free exchange of ideas, the vigorous debates, and even the disagreements, provided they were expressed openly, honestly, and charitably. He himself was in a listening mode, as demanded by synodality, and he encouraged his brother bishops to open their minds and hearts to the promptings of the Holy Spirit expressed in the mutual dialogue.

Campus ministers do well to reflect deeply on the remarkable address of Pope Francis on the fiftieth anniversary of the establishment of the Synod of Bishops. Inspired by Francis, we can imagine some possible features of a synodal church on campus. All the members think of themselves as both teachers and learners. The professional campus ministers see themselves as servants of the community. They create an atmosphere that encourages creativity and initiative among all members. They spot talented people, help them develop their gifts, and encourage them to use their talents for the common good. At regular staff meetings, the members can pray together; share their pastoral successes as well as their personal frustrations; do faith sharing on the Sunday readings; discuss common projects; get advice on personal responsibilities; and engage in informal conversation over a shared meal. Important controversial decisions and problems are discussed in public sessions open to all members. Dialogue is celebrated and practiced with special emphasis on developing listening skills. The pastoral staff periodically gets away for fun and recreation. The pastor prepares for his homilies by meeting with small groups to discuss the Sunday readings. Energy centers develop around groups with passionate concerns, and leaders promote a synergistic pluralism rather than a safe uniformity.

A synodal church on campus is not turned in on itself, totally consumed by internal affairs. Following the lead of Francis, it participates in dialogue and collaboration with other religious groups on campus. It keeps alive the prayer of Jesus that all his followers remain united as one flock under one shepherd. These general perspectives, drawn from the synodal theology and practice of Pope Francis, can generate creative programming for campus ministry now and in the future.

V

APPROPRIATING THE FAITH

10

STRIVING
FOR RELIGIOUS LITERACY

The ministerial function of appropriating the faith enables Catholics to achieve a mature understanding of their faith so they can give effective witness to the gospel and deal with the challenges to belief encountered in the academic world. The goal is a faith that fosters a deeper personal commitment to Christ and a more enlightened practice of Christian discipleship in the world. The pastoral letter *Empowered by the Spirit* emphasizes the positive role of theology in keeping alive the great questions of meaning, purpose, and identity and in producing a coherent vision of life centered on Christ. Campus ministers have the responsibility of creating a learning community where all the members can deepen their understanding of their faith.

In this chapter, based on a publication in 2000,[1] we summarize the kinds of attitudes, skills, and knowledge that educated Catholics need to live effectively in the contemporary world. The ideas presented serve as a useful guide for campus ministers designing religious education programs.

CATHOLIC GRADUATES AND RELIGIOUS LITERACY

It is helpful to address the question of the theological education of collegians by focusing on the kinds of attitudes, skills, and knowledge that adult Catholics need in today's world. This is valuable in determining how we best carry out the ministerial function of appropriating the faith. By imagining the ideal outcome of this effort, we prepare for the practical question of how we can perform this ministerial task more effectively.

Sketching a portrait of a theologically educated Catholic is complicated by the legitimate pluralism that exists in the Catholic community. We have diverse outlooks on many pertinent questions: for instance, how Catholics relate to American society and which theological school should guide our efforts to pass on the Catholic heritage. The following suggestions are heavily influenced by the thought of Karl Rahner, SJ, keeping in mind alternatives and correctives suggested by liberation theology and the work of Hans Urs von Balthasar.

ATTITUDES

1. *Valuable resource.* Catholic graduates should see their Catholic faith as a valuable resource for understanding the great questions of life and for living as responsible, mature, committed persons. Catholicism is not an enslaving, dehumanizing system as the classic critics Feuerbach, Marx, Nietzsche, and Freud claimed, but a liberating and empowering way of life. We want the Catholics formed at our campus centers to treasure their faith and to be passionate about passing it on to their children as a pearl of immense value.

2. *Lifelong process.* They should be committed to a lifelong process of deepening their understanding of their faith so that they can grow ever closer to Christ. We must help them recognize their need for an adult understanding of their faith to live as effective Christians in the contemporary world. Adapting the terminology of Jacques Maritain, we could say they need not only "tender hearts" that reflect the compassion of Jesus, but also "tough minds" that enable them to apply Christian principles to complex situations.

3. *Comprehensive way of life.* They should view their Catholic faith as a comprehensive, organic wisdom synthesis and not as a disparate collection of doctrines, rituals, and laws. It is a total way of life that touches all aspects of human existence; a symbol system in which all the components are organically connected; a complete package that has a clear focal point in commitment to Christ as the definitive prophet, the absolute savior, the Son of God. Our graduates should see how the various dogmas and doctrines, the liturgical practices and devotions, the institutional structures and laws all point to and find

their meaning in Jesus of Nazareth who revealed the secrets of God and sent the Spirit to guide us to all truth.

SKILLS

1. *Reading the Scriptures.* Adult Catholics should be able to read the Bible with a receptive heart and critical mind. The Bible is the word of God, the privileged witness to Jesus the Son of God, the normative guide for the ongoing life of the church. It is also the book of the church, produced by members of the community of faith. Modern biblical criticism helps us read the Scriptures more intelligently by emphasizing the historical and cultural context of the times, the intent of the authors, and the literary form they employed. More recently, literary approaches to the Bible have helped us better understand the internal structures of the various books and their narrative qualities.

2. *Positive role of theology.* Catholic graduates should have a positive appreciation of theology as a valuable guide for living the gospel and understanding their religious heritage. Anselm's description of theology as "faith seeking understanding" draws all believers into this essential task. Theology provides an approach and framework for wrestling with the great questions of life. It helps us to correlate the meanings and values of the Christian tradition with the meanings and values of our culture. Karl Rahner insisted that the more scientific theology is (that is, the more open to the questions of the day and the more knowledgeable about the Christian tradition), the more pastorally and spiritually relevant it will be. This new millennium is enriched by the valuable work done by the twentieth century theological giants Karl Rahner, Bernard Lonergan, and Hans Urs von Balthasar. Collectively, they have demonstrated that theology has many useful functions: keeping alive the memory of Jesus; refocusing and reinterpreting the vast Christian tradition; enabling us to think systematically about our faith; helping us avoid serious distortions in our understanding of the Catholic heritage; guiding our spiritual quest; and helping us work intelligently on the task of transforming the world. Graduates who appreciate the positive role of theology are more likely to accept the lifelong task of understanding their faith in greater depth.

3. *Faith and Scripture.* Educated Catholics should be able to defend their faith against the attacks of both secularists and fundamentalists. Against the rationalism spawned by the Enlightenment, we

must vindicate our religious claim that the human spirit is essentially open to the transcendent and is in danger of suffocation in a one-dimensional world. To deal effectively with Christian fundamentalists, who fight modernity with a questionable theory of biblical inerrancy and often manifest an anti-Catholic bias, a solid understanding of the Bible and some knowledge of legitimate ways of interpreting it is necessary. We should remain open to dialogue with fundamentalists based on charity and confidence in the Catholic approach to scripture.

4. *Theological reflection.* They should be able to do theological reflection both personally and in small groups. Theological reflection makes explicit the ordinary process of relating Christian tradition and daily experience in a search for a deeper understanding of both. Typically, the process begins by focusing on some aspect of personal experience; for example, a significant encounter with another person or in a primary activity, such as work. It is important to recognize the societal and cultural context of the experience; for instance, the ordinary patterns of male/female interactions in the United States. The second step is to describe or narrate the experience carefully and authentically, while bracketing traditional ways of interpreting it and avoiding premature judgments about it. The third step is to reflect on the experience in the light of the Christian tradition. This can be done in a variety of ways: reflecting on a Bible story with similar dynamics; asking what image of God or what mix of sin and grace is implied; thinking of how a saint handled a comparable situation; or recalling what theologians have said about it. Finally, the reflection should lead to some new praxis or informed change of behavior based on a transformed outlook. Students who have learned some process of theological reflection have a lifelong resource for deepening and applying their faith.

5. *Diversity and pluralism.* In this age of great societal change and complexity, Catholics must be able to deal constructively with the pluralism within the church. Since Vatican II, we have become more aware of diversity within the church. Theologically, we have at least three vibrant sources of theological reflection: the transcendental Thomists, represented by Karl Rahner and Bernard Lonergan; the liberationists, which include Latin Americans like Gustavo Gutierrez and feminists ranging from Rosemary Radford Ruether to Elizabeth Johnson; and the followers of the Swiss scholar Hans Urs von Balthasar. Avery Dulles has identified four different ways that Catholics relate to American society: traditionalists who want to revive a pre–Vatican II Catholicism in

order to fight against the culture of death, represented especially by the abortion mentality in our country; neoconservatives who celebrate our democratic capitalist system, but want to follow the lead of Pope John Paul II in fighting the culture war for the soul of America; liberals who want the church to learn from the American tradition of freedom and democracy and to push for greater social justice based on the consistent ethic of life; and radicals who oppose the violence and materialism in our country based on the gospel ideals of compassion, forgiveness, and nonviolence. Diverse pieties are also evident, ranging from traditionalists who prefer Latin Masses and want to reform the liturgical reforms, to charismatics who celebrate the gifts of the Spirit, and progressives who want greater cultural adaptation. It is crucial that our students learn to celebrate legitimate pluralism and avoid destructive polarization. The Common Ground statement, "Called to be Catholic: The Church in a Time of Peril," makes important suggestions for avoiding polarization and the paralysis that it engenders. We must accept Jesus Christ as the "measure without measure," and remain accountable to the Catholic tradition. Dialogue is our indispensable tool for dealing with disagreements. Effective dialogue is based on certain principles: remember that no particular group in the church has a monopoly on the truth or the right to spurn other Catholics; presume that others are acting in good faith; put the best possible interpretation on the opinion of others; do not impugn the loyalty of others; bring "fresh eyes, open minds and changed hearts" to the conversation. We need graduates who can participate in constructive dialogues on all the issues that divide Catholics.

6. *Openness to dialogue.* Catholics should be able to participate in interreligious and ecumenical dialogues based on confident commitment to their Catholic heritage and a general knowledge of other religious traditions. The Second Vatican Council spoke positively about the world religions as vehicles of grace and truth. With the mystical traditions of India—Hinduism and Buddhism—we share an appreciation of meditation for enlightenment. With the wisdom traditions of China—Confucianism and Taoism—we seek more harmonious ways of living. With the prophetic traditions of Judaism and Islam, Christians share a belief in one God who created the world and guides the historical journey of the human family. We Catholics join with the Orthodox, Anglican, and Protestant Christians in the effort to be more

151

faithful disciples of Jesus Christ and more effective instruments of the kingdom.

Over the last three decades, theologians have been engaged in formal dialogue with other Christians and have made remarkable progress in forging agreements on most long-disputed topics, such as justification and the real presence in the Eucharist. Interfaith dialogue searches for common ground, which is crucial for the well-being of the human family. As theologian Hans Kung states: "No peace among the nations without peace among the religions. No peace among the religions without dialogue between the religions."[2] Interreligious dialogue is not a luxury for a few intellectuals, but a responsibility for all who want to promote peace and harmony in the world.

7. *Unity in diversity.* Given the evident pluralism, it is very important that our graduates recognize the distinctive features of Catholicism. Being Catholic is a way of being human, religious, theistic, and Christian. We share a passion for personal development with humanists; a sense of mystery with religious people; a belief in one God with Jews and Muslims; and commitment to Christ with Orthodox Christians, Anglicans, and Protestants. But Catholicism presents a distinctive, if not unique, profile. At the core of Catholic sensibilities is the incarnational outlook, or sacramental principle, which recognizes that the infinite God is present in our finite world. We inhabit one graced world. All things are potentially revelatory. Jesus Christ is present in the assembly gathered for worship and in the consecrated bread and wine. The beauty of our created world and the goodness in the human heart reflect the Source of all beauty and goodness. This core conviction gives Catholics a positive sense of human nature and the material world. Our graduates should understand and appreciate how regular participation in the Eucharist inculcates and enriches the incarnational perspective on life.

Additionally, Catholicism engenders other convictions and sensibilities: a recognition of the importance of the Petrine Office as a focal point of unity and a beacon for gospel values; an appreciation of the long, rich, and diverse Christian tradition that is indeed catholic, or universal; a positive outlook on human reason and the value of dialogue with philosophy and other disciplines such as psychology, sociology, and history. At its best, the Catholic tradition fosters a sense of unity-in-diversity. We, though many, are one body because we share the one loaf and drink from the same cup (cf. Rom 12:5). We may have diverse theologies and pieties, but we are united in dedication to Christ and accountability to Christ and the Christian tradition. Our goal is not uniformity, but solidarity in the quest for truth, goodness, and beauty. The Catholic imagination resonates with the traditional aphorism: in essentials unity; in accidentals freedom; and in all things charity. Catholicism has generally opted for "both-and" over the more distinctively Protestant "either-or." We have affirmed both Scripture and Tradition, both faith and reason, both grace and nature. As Aquinas insisted, grace builds on nature and does not destroy it. Catholics who differ on theological perspectives and concrete moral applications often can find unity in these essential Catholic sensibilities.

8. *Enlightened simplicity.* Catholics today need an enlightened simplicity that enables them to pass on their mature faith to the next generation in ways that are intelligible, credible, and appealing.

9. *Summary of belief.* Catholic graduates should be able to compose a short creed summarizing their beliefs as Christians.

10. *Resources.* They should be familiar with the resources for finding answers to questions that arise: for example, *Catechism of the Catholic Church; An Introduction to the New Testament* by Raymond Brown; *Catholicism* by Richard McBrien; *Compendium of Catholic Social Teaching;* the *Catholic Study Bible; The New Dictionary of Theology* edited by Joseph Komonchak; and *Vatican Council II: The Conciliar and Post-Conciliar Documents* edited by Austin Flannery.

KNOWLEDGE

1. *Knowledge of Scripture.* Catholic graduates should have a working knowledge of the Bible. They should be aware that the seventy-two books of the Bible (forty-five in the Hebrew Scriptures and twenty-seven in the New Testament) were written by various authors in different historical periods, using a variety of literary forms. They should know the main outline of biblical history: the exodus under Moses around the thirteenth century BC; the gradual conquest of Palestine during the next few centuries; the establishment and solidification of the monarchy under Saul, David, and Solomon at the beginning of the new millennium; the subsequent series of wars with foreign invaders, including the Assyrian conquest of the northern kingdom in 721 BC; the Babylonian capture and destruction of Jerusalem in 586 BC, and the return from exile in 539 BC; the Greek conquest of Palestine

under Alexander the Great in 332 BC; and, finally, the Roman occupation in 63 BC, which lasted throughout the New Testament period and includes another destruction of Jerusalem in AD 70. Students should know the stories of the great figures of the Hebrew Scriptures: the ancestors of the Israelites Abraham and Sarah, Isaac and Rebekah, Jacob and Rachel; the great liberator Moses; the judges, such as Samson and Samuel; the kings, especially David and Solomon; and the great prophetic figures Elijah, Isaiah, Jeremiah, and Ezekiel.

Turning to the New Testament, adult Catholics should recognize the importance of the Apostle Paul, and know some of the major themes of his letters; for instance, that we are members of the Body of Christ and should live in charity with one another. They should have confidence that the four Gospels give us a substantially correct picture of the historical Jesus, and that they enrich our understanding of the Lord by presenting him from diverse perspectives. Catholics should know something about the distinctive literary form known as apocalyptic literature, found in the Book of Revelation.

2. *The Second Vatican Council.* Educated Catholics should have a clear understanding of the spirit and main teachings of the Second Vatican Council. For those graduating now, the Council is a historical event and not a remembered transforming experience as it is for some campus ministers. However, our students must know about Vatican II because it continues to guide the life of the church today. From 1962 to 1965, over three thousand bishops from around the world met and, with the help of theological experts, produced sixteen documents. Some of the documents reflect unresolved conflicts between conservative and progressive bishops, meaning that there are passages that can be used to support opposed positions today. Graduates should know the major directions taken by the Council: full active participation in the liturgy; participation of all the baptized in the universal priesthood of Christ; the co-responsibility of Christians for the church; the responsibility of the laity for transforming the world; the great importance of the scriptures as the normative witness to divine revelation; the encouragement of ecumenical dialogue; and an optimistic understanding of salvation based on divine love and fidelity to conscience.

3. *Catholic Social Teaching.* Graduates should know the main themes of the social teaching of the church and be able to apply it to concrete contemporary issues. Modern Catholic social teaching began in 1891, when Pope Leo XIII published his famous encyclical

Rerum Novarum, which presents a Catholic perspective on important social issues, such as the right of workers to form unions. In dialoguing with the modern world, Leo XIII opened the way to a developing body of Catholic social teaching, including important papal documents: *Quadragesimo Anno* (1931), in which Pius XI proposes the principle of subsidiarity; *Pacem in Terris* (1963), in which John XXIII defends human rights and calls for world peace; *Octagesimo Adveniens* (1971), in which Paul VI recognizes the importance of political liberation as well as economic development; *Centesimus Annus* (1991), in which John Paul II examines the strengths and weaknesses of capitalism and the free market; *Caritas in Veritate* (2009), in which Benedict XVI insists that both charity and truth are needed for integral human development; and *Laudato Si'* (2015), in which Pope Francis calls for an integral ecology concerned with environmental degradation and human suffering. The Second Vatican Council made an important contribution to Catholic social thought through its *Pastoral Constitution on the Church in the Modern World* (*Gaudiuim et Spes*), which addresses a wide variety of issues ranging from family life to nuclear weapons. Throughout the twentieth century, the Catholic Bishops of the United States have addressed the social questions facing the country. Of special note are their pastoral letters, *The Challenge of Peace* (1983) and *Economic Justice for All* (1986), which serve as excellent models for Catholic approaches to critical issues facing the country.

At the heart of Catholic social thought is a recognition of the essential worth of every human being and the conviction that persons flourish in stable families, just economies, and a peaceful world. Our graduates should appreciate this core conviction and know that church leaders have used it to develop an impressive body of social doctrine that can guide our involvement in the public life of the country.

4. Communion of Saints. In a culture struggling to find role models, our graduates should be familiar with the saints and spiritual leaders who give a human face to Catholic ideals. From that immense cloud of witnesses we recall: the mystics, John of the Cross and Teresa of Avila; the reformers, Catherine of Siena and Francis de Sales; the popes, Gregory the Great and John XXIII; the doctors of the church, Jerome and Therese of Lisieux; the martyrs, Edith Stein and Oscar Romero; the American spiritual leaders, Dorothy Day and Thomas Merton; founders of orders, Francis and Clare of Assisi, Dominic Guzman, Ignatius of Loyola, Jane Frances de Chantal, and Mother Teresa.

5. *Major Theologians.* Educated Catholics should know the great theologians who have developed new paradigms for articulating the Christian faith: the Apostle Paul, who insisted on justification through faith; the Evangelist John, who presented Jesus and the Paraclete as the source of truth and life; Origen, who articulated Christian faith in terms of Neoplatonic philosophy; Augustine, who rethought Christianity in the wake of the fall of Rome; Bonaventure, who set a framework for a spiritual theology based on vestiges of the Trinity in the world and human consciousness; Aquinas, who incorporated Aristotelian philosophy into a Christian framework; Karl Rahner, who reinterpreted the Christian tradition in a modern context; and Hans Urs von Balthasar, who refocused the Christian tradition on beauty. It is also important to recognize the impressive growing body of work by women theologians: for example, the books by Elizabeth Johnson, including *She Who Is* and *The Quest for the Living God.*

6. *Church History.* Educated Catholics should have a general knowledge of the broad outline of church history: the production of the New Testament during the first century after the death of Jesus; the Roman persecutions from AD 64 under Nero until the early fourth century; the conversion of Constantine and the granting of a privileged position to Christianity in the Roman Empire; the rise of monasticism, first in the East and then in the West, especially in the sixth century under the influence of St. Benedict; the official split between the Eastern and Western churches in 1054; the creation of the great theological syntheses during the Middle Ages, especially by Aquinas in the thirteenth century; the Protestant Reformation in the sixteenth century followed by the Council of Trent and reform within the Catholic Church; the First Vatican Council in 1870; and the development in the twentieth century, including the ecumenical movement and the charismatic renewal.

7. *Major Areas of Theology.* Educated Catholics require a fundamental knowledge of the major areas of theology: a Christian anthropology that recognizes we are interdependent creatures with a positive orientation to the Creator of life; a doctrine of God that understands the transcendent God is present in the world and is the ultimate source of our capacity for knowledge and love; a theology of grace that knows we are temples of the Holy Spirit, who is more powerful than all the dark forces; a theology of revelation that appreciates that all finite realities are potentially revelatory of the Infinite; a soteriology that emphasizes that

God grants the grace of salvation to those who faithfully follow their conscience; a Christology that sees Jesus as the parable of the Father and the paradigm of fulfilled humanity; an ecclesiology that celebrates the church as the communion of baptized believers and the sacrament of the risen Lord; a moral theology that is centered on the love of God and neighbor; a sacramentology that understands the sacraments, and especially the Eucharist, as actualizations of the life of the church and privileged encounters with the risen Christ; and an eschatology that hopes for a final positive completion of the historical process and the ultimate fulfillment of the longings of the human heart in the life of heaven where God is all in all.

DIALOGUE WITH FRANCIS

Pope Francis is not a professional theologian like his predecessor Pope Benedict. He did the standard courses in the seminary but did not earn a doctorate in theology. He often says that for him, facts are more important than ideas. His typical style is to respond to situations and questions with pastoral advice rather than dogmatic statements. To a young girl in the Philippines asking why she has had so much suffering in her life from hunger and homelessness, Francis responded not with an abstract summary of a theology of evil but with the empathetic comment that some things in life can only be seen with eyes cleansed by tears.

Nevertheless, Francis is in dialogue with the world of theology and has some distinctive insights that can enrich campus ministry. His Christian anthropology is strongly communal, stressing our relationship to God, to other humans, especially the marginalized, and to the natural world, which provides a solid warrant for programs promoting social justice and environmental protection. For the pope, God is the Creator who calls us to cooperate in the ongoing work of creation and the One who never tires of forgiving us—important notions for collegians groping their way through their formative years. Christ is a person, like us in all things but sin, who remains our companion throughout our entire journey of life. This faith conviction can help collegians prepare well for the challenges of the next phase of their lives.

The pope's distinctive image of the church as a field hospital reminds campus ministers of their responsibility to be present on campus, ready to attend to the most seriously wounded. Francis speaks of the eucharistic liturgy as "an act of cosmic love," which could help the church on campus avoid a ghetto mentality, by reminding worshippers of their fundamental relationships with the academic community, the diocesan and universal church, the Communion of Saints, and with the whole cosmos. The way Francis places moral prohibitions within the larger context of Christ's law of love gives campus ministers a way of avoiding divisive culture wars while concentrating on the love of God and neighbor that brings Catholics together. Finally, the pope's eschatological conviction that the whole of creation will share in the final victory can encourage the church on campus to take concrete action to protect the environment, such as reducing the use of paper and plastic products, turning off lights, and conserving water.

Although Francis is not a professional theologian, he has appropriated and popularized elements of the Catholic theological tradition that can help the church on campus to be a more effective witness to the teachings of Christ.

Pope Francis also reminds us of the potential power of liturgical preaching to facilitate the entire process of appropriating the faith. In *The Joy of the Gospel*, he provides us with a masterful treatment of the homily and effective preparation for preaching (n. 135–59). It is important to understand the nature and function of the homily in the context of the Eucharistic liturgy. It is not a speech or a lecture, nor is it primarily "a time for meditation and catechesis." It is best understood as a special moment in the ongoing dialogue initiated by God with his people, which proclaims "the great deeds of salvation" and restates "the demands of the covenant" (n. 137). To preach effectively, the homilist must be close to the people and understand their heart, a point supported by research that identifies the statement "the preacher understands my heart" as one of the highest predictors of perceived sermon effectiveness.[3] Making a point no doubt welcomed by many Catholics, Francis insists that the homily should be brief because if it "goes on too long," it disrupts the balance and rhythm of the liturgy. In a typical use of family experience, the pope suggests that a homily should be like a mother speaking to her child based on a relationship of love and trust. Recognizing God's grace at work in her children, she "listens to their concerns and learns from them" (n. 139). Similarly, the good preacher knows the heart of the people and appreciates their culture as "a source of living water." This enables the homilist to speak in the "mother culture" of the assembly using language that is like music that "inspires encouragement, strength and enthusiasm" (n. 139). A liturgical preacher can encourage the dialogue between the Lord and his people by "the warmth of his tone of voice, the unpretentiousness of his manner of speaking, the joy of his gestures," even if his homily "may be somewhat tedious" (n. 140).

Examining the secret that made Jesus such an effective preacher able to attract "ordinary people by his lofty teachings and demands," Francis identifies the way he "looked at people, seeing beyond their weakness and failings." Filled with the Spirit, he enjoyed "talking with the people" and encouraging them not to fear because they are loved by the Father (n. 141). Homilists should learn from Christ, drawing on the beauty of his imagery to reveal the truth and "encourage the practice of the good." Effective preaching has "a quasi-sacramental character," enhancing the personal dialogue between Christ and the hearers of the word of Scripture, which is "a gift before it is a demand" (n. 142).

Expanding on his fundamental conviction that good homilies enhance the dialogue between "God and His people," the pope speaks of "enculturated preaching" that proclaims not abstracted ideas or detached values but "a synthesis" that strengthens the divine-human covenant and "consolidates the bond of charity." In our ordinary lives, we speak directly to God in "a thousand ways," but in the homily "believers keep silence and allow God to speak" while the homilist expresses their feelings, so that afterward all the hearers of the preached word can continue the conversation in their own way (n. 143). This profound analysis of how a good homily functions highlights the role of the preacher as a mediator of the ongoing dialogue between Christ and his followers.

Francis also offers his thoughts on preparing homilies, insisting that "a sufficient portion of personal and community time be dedicated to this task, even if this means less time for other important activities. He makes his point with the striking indictment that a preacher who does not prepare is "dishonest and irresponsible with the gifts he has received" (n. 145). Proper preparation requires attention to the biblical texts with "reverence for the truth," which recognizes that we are servants of the scriptures, not masters. We should approach the biblical texts with "undivided attention," "serious concentration," and "a holy fear," lest we distort their meaning (n. 146). The goal is to discover the "central message" of the assigned liturgical texts, which includes the meaning and effect intended by the author. Francis exemplifies this point in a series of striking admonitions that, if heeded, would dramatically improve preaching. "If a text was written to console, it should not be used to correct errors; if it was written as an exhortation, it should not be employed to teach doctrine; if it was written to teach something about God, it should not be used to expound various theological opinions; if it was written as a summons to praise or missionary outreach, let us not use it to talk about the latest news" (n. 147). We should interpret individual texts both in the light of the general thrust of the biblical teaching and in its "distinct and specific emphasis" (n. 148).

Francis encourages preachers to "personalize the word" by approaching the scriptures "with a docile and prayerful heart" so that the biblical word penetrates our thoughts and feelings. He links this process with homily effectiveness: "The Sunday readings will resonate in all their brilliance in the hearts of the faithful if they have first done so in the heart of their pastor" (n. 149). The pope recommends that preachers regularly engage in *lectio divina*, a prayerful encounter with the scriptural text open to ways it conveys a personal message from the Lord. He suggests we ask ourselves, "Lord, what does this text say to me? What is it about my life that you want to change by this text? What troubles me about this text? Why am I not interested in this? Or perhaps: What do I find pleasant in this text? What is it about this word that moves me? What attracts me? Why does it attract me?" (n. 153).

In a profoundly insightful and eminently practical passage, Francis insists that preachers must contemplate not only the scriptures but also their people, paying attention to their aspirations and limitations; their "ways of praying, of loving, of looking at life and the world;" and to "their language, their signs and symbols" as well as the questions they ask (n. 154). The preacher's task is "to link the message of a biblical text to a human situation, to an experience which cries out for the light of God's word" (n. 154). This requires a "spiritual sensitivity for reading God's message in events" grounded in an "evangelical discernment" that recognizes God's call resounding in the historical situation (n. 154).

Preachers should not respond to questions nobody asks, but should "develop a broad and profound sensitivity to what really affects other people's lives," attentive to "ordinary human experiences such as a joyful reunion, a moment of disappointment, the fear of being alone, compassion at the sufferings of others, uncertainty about the future, concern for a loved one, and so forth" (n. 155). In addressing such issues, homilists are more effective if they use concrete examples and attractive images that seem "familiar, close to home, practical, and related to everyday life" (n. 157). Avoiding esoteric theological terms, effective preachers use simple language understood by the people and construct homilies that are clear and easy to follow. Francis concludes his advice for preachers by emphasizing the power of "positive preaching" that puts more emphasis on "what can be done better than on what should not be done." Positive preaching does not get "mired in complaints, laments, criticisms, and reproaches," but offers "hope and points to the future" (n. 159).

Those who preach in campus churches are well advised to implement the sage advice offered by Pope Francis in *The Joy of the Gospel*. For example: reflect prayerfully on the assigned scripture texts open to a personal message from the Lord; listen to students and faculty members and be alert to their common human concerns; correlate the intended meaning of the texts with the concerns of the members of the faith community; use language and images familiar to students that gain attention and further the main point; put more emphasis on spiritual growth than moral prohibitions; and proclaim a message of hope that helps the community face the challenges of the academic world. On residential campuses where Sunday liturgies draw good crowds, preachers who serve the community full time can draw on their interactions with students to preach homilies that are relevant to their real-life concerns. Churches on campus that do not have a resident priest should make every effort to invite priests who are good homilists or who will allow staff members to preach or give witness talks. Most good homilies are not directly didactic, but all preaching guided by Francis can help the church on campus carry out its ministerial task of appropriating the faith.

11

ENDOWED PROFESSORSHIPS

This chapter describes the establishment of a professorship in Catholic thought at the University of Toledo to encourage campus ministers around the country to do something similar on their respective campus.[1] Since its establishment, the professorship has become "The Thomas and Margaret Murray and James J. Bacik Chair of Catholic Studies," thanks to a generous gift from the Lovell Foundation in 2001. Dr. Richard Gaillardetz, who later served as president of the Catholic Theological Society of America, held the chair for ten years during which time the University established a major in religious studies and a Center for Religious Understanding, which sponsors an annual Jewish Christian Muslim Dialogue and monthly interfaith discussions for students. Dr. Gaillardetz served as a public voice for the Catholic tradition, giving lectures, doing numerous media interviews, writing op-ed pieces for the local paper, participating in interfaith dialogues, publishing numerous books and articles, and serving on university committees. After his departure from Toledo in 2010 for an endowed chair at Boston College, the Murray Bacik Chair has been held by Dr. Peter Feldmeier, who has found his own ways of publicly representing the Catholic tradition; for example, serving for a time as the Sunday homilist for *America* magazine.

Based on this initiative and experience, I have made myself available as a consultant for campus ministers interested in establishing Catholic chairs at their universities. Some of those consultations occurred informally at conferences or through a series of phone conversations. In other situations, campus ministers invited me to their campuses for more formal conversations. For example, with the help of a respected Catholic faculty member at the University of New Mexico in Albuquerque, I met with university officials, making the case for a Chair in Catholic Studies and sharing with them examples of contracts negotiated at other universities that successfully dealt with church and state issues. I also participated in a daylong meeting with the local bishop and some of his priests where we discussed the advantages of a Catholic chair, how to protect the church's interests while respecting the legitimate rights of the university, and how to raise the $2 million needed for the endowment. Eventually, the university and the diocese reached a mutually satisfying agreement, establishing the Endowed Chair of Roman Catholic Studies in the Religious Studies program. Chairs also have been established at the University of Kentucky and the University of Cincinnati with similar dynamics. Despite changing circumstances, my hope is that some enterprising campus ministers will be encouraged by this article to do something similar on their campuses. Such an initiative is a wonderful way to move campus ministry from the periphery to the center of academic life and bring the Catholic intellectual tradition into the public forum.

STRATEGIES FOR ESTABLISHING CATHOLIC CHAIRS

In February of 1992, the Catholic community at the University of Toledo, a state institution, officially established the Margaret and Thomas Murray Professorship in Catholic Thought, funded by the highly respected trial lawyer, Thomas Murray, to honor his parents. The professorship, located in the College of Arts and Sciences, was established to attract a visiting expert in the Catholic Tradition to the University of Toledo for one academic term each year. This professor would teach two courses during the term and give an open lecture to the public. The courses taught are for full academic credit and deal with some recognized aspect of the Roman Catholic tradition. The dean of the College of Arts and Sciences will appoint an annual search committee to choose a candidate and the person will be appointed to the position in accordance with the general procedures of the university.

While the proposal outlined below clearly applies to public institutions such as state universities and city colleges as well as private secular institutions, it may also apply to some private institutions with denominational ties.

THE CONCEPT

To establish a full-time chair or visiting professorship, the Catholic community on campus must first initiate an effort to raise a substantial amount of money—over $1 million for a full-time chair or around $500,000 for a visiting professorship—as an endowment to the university. The interest from the endowment is used to pay for a permanent or visiting professor who teaches courses in some aspect of the Catholic tradition. According to current policies at the University of Toledo, our $500,000 generates 5 percent a year toward the professorship. The university uses 3 percent to increase the principal to maintain its purchasing power over the years and 2 percent to pay for administrative expenses. A contract needs to be drawn up so that the interests of the Catholic community and the university can both be protected. Universities generally insist on total control of the endowment fund. In our contract with the University of Toledo, we protected our interests in numerous ways. One clause, for example, states that the holder of the professorship be "a recognized scholar in the Catholic tradition."

We chose to establish our professorship on a visiting basis so that someone new would come each year for one academic term. This enabled us to begin with a fund of $500,000. In some situations, campus ministers may decide that having a permanent full-time occupant of a chair is more desirable. Today, that requires an initial endowment of over $1 million. In 1990, the University of Rochester, a private secular university, established the John Henry Newman Professorship in Roman Catholic Studies, with an endowment of one million dollars.

THE RATIONALE

To help collegians meet current challenges to their faith and to prepare them for future leadership roles in society and church, more Catholic professorships are needed.

Many collegians are in a process of moving from a naïve adolescent belief system to an adult appropriation of their faith. The academic world provides catalysts and challenges. In the classroom, students learn to question traditional assumptions and encounter the modern critics of religion who claim it is either infantile or dehumanizing. On campus, they meet peers who hold divergent world views, including fundamentalist Christians who aggressively challenge members of mainline churches. Unfortunately, many Catholic students are poorly prepared to deal with intellectual challenges to their faith. They do not have sufficient knowledge of their religious heritage to speak about it with an understanding that matches their convictions.

These collegians are victims of the general religious illiteracy that impoverishes our society. As a nation, we know too little of the religious wellsprings of Western culture and the distinctive ways the Judeo-Christian tradition has shaped our national life. Public education in the United States has failed to pass on the religious heritage. There is little sense that a well-rounded education should include a religious component. Many colleges and universities do not have departments or programs of religious studies. Some academics still think that teaching about religions necessarily involves proselytizing.

Significant efforts are being made at the collegiate level to meet the challenge of religious illiteracy. Some state universities have excellent departments of religion or religious studies programs that enable students to gain a broad understanding of various religious traditions. Schools with denominational ties usually offer opportunities to study their heritage in greater depth. Many Catholic colleges and universities committed to passing on their tradition have made significant improvements in their theology offerings in recent years.

Campus ministers try to meet the challenge by providing a variety of noncredit courses, lectures, and seminars. A few campus ministers at state schools have found creative ways of offering credit courses by arranging credit transfers with local Catholic colleges. The Catholic Archdiocese of Denver sponsors a Theologian-in-Residence Program, which provides the resources of a professional theologian for the University of Northern Colorado and Colorado State University as well as credit courses for the students.

Some private institutions, including Harvard, Yale, Case Western and the Universities of Chicago, Tulsa, and Rochester, have Catholic chairs. The visiting professorship at Tulsa established in 1986 is part of the William K. Warren Center for Catholic Studies, which also includes a public lecture series. The University of Pittsburgh, a state-related institution, has a Catholic chair endowed with over $1 million that is currently being filled on a visiting basis, but will eventually fund a full-time, tenured professor. Some Catholic institutions have endowed positions such as the Laurence J. McGinley chair at Fordham and the John A. O'Brien professorships at Notre Dame.

A few state universities have creative arrangements for Catholic Studies. Recently, the University of Illinois developed a renewable position jointly appointed and funded by the Religious Studies Program of the university and the Newman Foundation for a professor who teaches one course for the university's program and a credit course in the "courses offered by religious foundations" program. For over sixty years, the Newman Foundation has offered courses in Catholic theology for which university credit is obtained. While taught in university classrooms for credit, the grades earned in the courses offered by the religious foundations do not count toward the computed grade point average.

The University of Iowa, which has had a Catholic Chair funded by the diocese since 1927, is moving toward making it an endowed position.

The University of Toledo now has the Margaret and Thomas Murray Professorship in Catholic Thought, which to my knowledge is the first endowed visiting professorship at a state university. Despite these efforts, religious illiteracy continues to be a problem and too many of our Catholic students remain ill-equipped for the challenges they face now and in the future. John Courtney Murray, SJ, argued many years ago that college students have a right to learn about their religious heritage. It is not only unhealthy but also unjust to deprive them of the opportunity to probe more deeply into the religious dimension of their own lives and the culture in which they live.

A constructive response to the rights and needs of our students is to establish more endowed professorships that offer credit courses in Catholic thought. The credit is crucial because busy students are more inclined to put their time and energy into credit courses than noncredit offerings. Campus ministry programs are always at a disadvantage in competing for students' time when it comes to academic requirements. Catholic professorships will help overcome this problem and thus serve as a more effective means of responding to religious illiteracy.

CREATING A MOVEMENT

Our experience at the University of Toledo convinces me that it is possible to do something similar at other institutions and that the effort will have great benefits for the church on campus. My intention is to motivate campus ministers who function in both the ecclesial and academic worlds to use their unique position to further this project.

We could imagine a few well-established campus ministers seizing the moment and rather quickly initiating a process of getting endowed positions established at their institutions. This could launch a national movement with an energy and momentum of its own. We would gradually accumulate experience on how best to accomplish this. A growing number of campus ministers would see the possibility of doing something similar. More affluent Catholics would recognize the value of supporting Catholic professorships as an effective way of serving the common good and expressing gratitude for their own good fortune. Theologians in the United States, and indeed around the world, would have more opportunities for exercising their ministries.

Successful professorships demonstrate to the academic world a continuing interest in religious matters and spur development of programs and courses in religious studies. Theology, in turn, gains academic respectability and Catholic students are given more opportunities to explore their heritage and to prepare themselves for future leadership. Other religious traditions would be moved to consider doing something similar. Through this entire process, campus ministry would make important strides in the ongoing struggle to move from the periphery to the very center of the academic world.

The scope of this dream may well exceed the realistic possibilities in our current situation. Surely, endowed professorships are not a panacea. Nevertheless, it is a project that at least some campus ministers can accomplish to the benefit of their institutions. If enough committed persons act on this proposal, the dream may materialize in the surprising ways that we often attribute to the work of the Spirit.

Drawing on our experience at the University of Toledo, the following suggestions are directed to campus ministers for establishing professorships at their institutions. Since situations vary greatly, these suggestions are intended as a catalyst for creative thinking.

ESTABLISHING A CORE GROUP

Campus ministers can begin by gathering a group of persons open to the project. It is helpful to include representatives of the ministerial staff, the Catholic community on campus, the academic community, and the public at large. Making use of this proposal, the group can discuss the general concept. It is useful to examine the bishops' pastoral letter on campus ministry, *Empowered by the Spirit*, especially the section dealing with appropriating the faith (n. 45–58), which includes the suggestion of "founding an endowed chair for Catholic Thought" (n. 57).

This discussion enables some of those who showed an initial interest to become enlightened and committed proponents of the professorship. Along with the campus ministers, they can form a core group or executive committee that will manage the many relationships and factors involved in the task and collaborate on getting more people committed to the project, especially individuals with needed skills and connections. They will have to determine the best ways of getting the support of the bishop of the diocese, involving the appropriate officials of the university, and informing the leaders of other religious traditions.

The committee can assess the political climate on campus, investigate policies on endowed professorships, and determine how to deal with the university bureaucracy. It can secure the services of a lawyer to draw up a contract and find appropriate ways to carry out the fundraising. Some of these tasks call for further comment.

THE BISHOP'S SUPPORT

It is essential to gain the support of the local bishop for the project and to do so early in the process. The faith community on campus is the local embodiment of the diocesan church led by the bishop. As the official teacher in the diocese, the bishop has a general responsibility for theological education. In the situation at the University of Toledo, the contract establishing the professorship was signed by the bishop. Any major fund-raising effort that goes beyond the university community may require the permission of the bishop.

Campus ministers can present the professorship to the bishop as an excellent way of reaching the undergraduate students and of gaining credibility for Catholic teaching.

This argument can be strengthened by placing it in the context of the great difficulty campus ministry centers around the country have had in overcoming religious illiteracy and in getting students involved in noncredit programs.

One major problem is that once the endowed position is established, the bishop no longer has control over the appointment of professors. At times, appointments may be made that displease the bishop. Given this realistic possibility, it must be argued that the overall good accomplished by the professorship will outweigh the potential problems created by questionable appointments.

Furthermore, there is the argument that it is unlikely that the university will want to offend the Catholic community by a series of unacceptable appointments. In the contract with the University of Toledo, we safeguarded our interests by including the clause, "The parties to this agreement understand that the Diocese of Toledo would welcome the opportunity to review and comment on such candidates." Given the church and state issue, it is not possible for the local bishop to maintain total control over the appointments. This must be faced realistically.

In the Diocese of Toledo, our bishops have a long history of supporting the efforts of campus ministry. Despite the potential problems, Bishop James Hoffman was immediately attuned to the value of the professorship and offered his complete support for our project. This was extremely important in our efforts to raise the endowment money. Our promotional material, which sought support not only for the professorship but also for a proposed religious studies center, prominently displayed the bishop's statement: "Today's collegians will be the leaders of tomorrow in our parishes and in our society. In order to meet their responsibilities, they need a solid understanding of their Catholic heritage. A Professorship in Catholic thought and a Religious Studies Center at the University of Toledo forms a creative response to this pressing problem."

RELATIONSHIP TO THE UNIVERSITY

Since universities benefit greatly from endowed professorships, they have an inherent interest in their establishment. Proposals for a Catholic professorship should meet with a positive response from University administrators, provided any lingering doubts about church and state relations are satisfied. We obtained a positive statement of support from the president of the University of Toledo, Frank E. Horton, which was used in our fund-raising campaign.

A key paragraph taken from his longer statement reads: "The proposed Professorship in Catholic Thought is especially welcomed by the University. I support this proposal since it will provide a valuable addition to our faculty and course offerings. I have every hope that such a Professorship will enable students to explore an important aspect of human culture in an objective and academically sound way under the guidance of outstanding visiting professors. I support this fund-raising project and look forward to the mutual benefits it will bring."

It is possible that some administrators or faculty members may be opposed to the establishment of a Catholic professorship for several reasons, including fear of church and state entanglement, excessive Catholic influence, proselytizing in the classroom, and the promotion of religious exclusivism. In response, it helps to emphasize that the professorship will be established according to all the proper academic procedures and norms and that the courses will encourage an objective and academically sound exploration of an important aspect of human culture. The support of the president and the inherent interest of the university in having endowed positions make it unlikely that opponents could ultimately block a proposal that follows the usual academic norms.

We found that having the support of individuals in key decision-making positions such as the Vice President for Academic Affairs, the Dean of the College of Arts and Sciences, and the Chair of the Philosophy Department greatly enhanced our ability to move our project forward.

We also made sure that some members of the Board of Trustees understood our proposal and would be prepared to support it if any troubles arose.

It is important to relate the establishment of the Catholic professorship to the existing offerings in religious studies. If there is a department or program, the appropriate chairs or coordinators must be brought into the discussion at an early stage. Efforts should be made to see that the professorship becomes an integral part of existing programs.

At the University of Toledo, there was not a Department of Religion or a Religious Studies Program. Therefore, we located our professorship in the College of Arts and Sciences under the authority of the

Dean so that the visiting scholars could be assigned to a department based on their area of expertise. At the same time, we encouraged the establishment of a religious studies program at the university. Since the university had no funds for hiring new professors, a professor in the philosophy department was encouraged to develop a proposal in which he would teach an introductory course on religious studies and then identify other courses already in the curriculum that could be used in building a religious studies major. The proposal includes a capstone project or paper in the senior year. This is the type of program that has been successfully run at the University of Michigan for many years. The director of our religious studies program now sees the establishment of the Catholic professorship as a helpful element in his overall plan. This is an example of trying to relate the Catholic professorship to the existing situation and to the ongoing needs of the university.

THE ECUMENICAL AND INTERFAITH DIMENSION

At the very outset of the process, leaders of other religious communities should be informed about the project. We not only disclosed our plan but also encouraged our friends in other traditions to consider establishing professorships in Judaic, Muslim, and Protestant thought. This presents an exciting possibility that would greatly enrich the intellectual life of the whole university and provide students with the opportunity to study other religious traditions.

Bringing the other communities into the discussion helps to diffuse criticism and can expand support for the general concept. In our situation, various campus ministers gathered some of their key supporters so that I could explain our project to them. This has sparked a continuing discussion of the possibility of establishing their own professorships. The results of this continuing discussion at the University of Toledo are not yet clear.

THE CONTRACT

We tried to obtain contracts for existing chairs at various universities but did not find anything very helpful. So, we gathered a group of interested university administrators and faculty members to discuss the general guidelines and assurances that should be in the contract. This included brainstorming on numerous ways in which the long-term

171

interests of the Catholic community might be at risk and how they could be protected. This material was then given to a lawyer to formulate a contract. Eventually, lawyers representing both the diocese and the university entered long and difficult discussions. The key problems from the university side were whether certain provisions of the proposed contract would involve church and state entanglements that could be challenged in the courts. In one clause, we had proposed that the person holding the professorship would ordinarily be Catholic, but that exceptions were possible. Although the university administration approved this formulation, the university lawyers did not. We eventually settled on the statement that the person chosen would be "a recognized scholar in the Roman Catholic tradition." Although the contract does not totally preclude the appointment of a critic of the Catholic Church or an individual with an anti-Catholic bias, it does give reasonable assurance that the visiting scholar will usually be a Catholic and that any exceptions will be persons who at least have a scholarly understanding of the Catholic tradition.

The other clause that caused some difficulty had to do with the desire of the diocese to have some say in the choice of the person for the professorship. An earlier draft stated that the Diocese of Toledo would have a representative on the search committee. During the discussion, this was softened to read that the Diocese of Toledo would welcome the opportunity to have a member on the search committee. Even this modified language was finally not acceptable to the university lawyers, and, after lengthy debate, we eventually settled on: "The dean of the College of Arts and Sciences shall have the authority to appoint a yearly search committee and may seek comment from the Diocese of Toledo about scholars who are candidates for the professorship. The parties to this agreement understand that the Diocese of Toledo would welcome the opportunity to review and comment on such candidates."

Currently, I am on the search committee and the cordial working relationships promise fruitful and agreeable results. The contract, however, must envision a changing situation and try to protect the interests of the Catholic community in the future.

One problem we envisioned was that an unsympathetic dean could scuttle the project by failing to appoint a search committee, thereby leaving the position unfilled. Thus, we included in the contract the clause: "Accordingly, the university agrees that if it fails to appoint a scholar to the professorship for three consecutive academic years, the endowment fund including principal and interest shall terminate and revert to its donor."

Ultimately, we are relying on a realistic assessment of the relationship between the local church and the university. It is our judgment that the university will not want to alienate the Catholic community by subverting the professorship or by making questionable appointments, especially since 42 percent of our student population is Catholic. Other situations where Catholics are more of a minority may require stricter contractual guarantees.

In speaking with legal experts not involved in our local negotiations, I have gained the impression that the university lawyers have been overly cautious in protecting against violations of church and state separation. It may be possible to negotiate contracts at other institutions that do a better job of protecting the interests of the Catholic community.

FUND-RAISING

Fr. Vince Krische, an extremely effective campus minister with rare fund-raising talents, suggests five components of successful development campaigns: Identifying potential donors, informing them about the project, involving them in the process, asking them for a specific gift, and recognizing their contributions.[2] Following his outline and suggestions, I want to offer some advice on raising money for a professorship.

The campaign should tap a wide variety of potential contributors, including faculty, administrators, staff, alumni, students and their parents, and members of the public with a special interest in the project. Establishing good lists of these various groups and continually expanding them is crucial. It is especially important to identify potential large contributors and to make a concerted effort to secure their support.

Such individuals contribute for diverse reasons. At one university, a major donor needed only a suggestion from a priest friend to redirect an intended charitable gift to the establishment of a Catholic chair. In our case, Tom and Ann Murray decided to make a sizeable contribution based on many factors. Tom, a well-known trial lawyer from Sandusky, Ohio, with wide-ranging interests and activities, including a very successful educational venture in Russia and two unsuccessful runs for Congress, wanted to honor his parents in a unique way. Since they had raised a large family and sacrificed to give them all a complete Catholic education, it seemed fitting to honor them by naming a professorship in Catholic thought after them. Tom and Ann, who are both committed to social causes and the common good, recognize the special importance of value-based education in today's complex, pluralistic culture. The professorship is a concrete way of making that kind of education more available to collegians at the University of Toledo. They are also enthusiastic about the broader implications of our project for Catholic education throughout the country. In short, funding the professorship corresponds to their deepest values and their pattern of Christian involvement in society.

There are many other individuals around the country like the Murrays who have been blessed financially and would find establishing a professorship a fitting way to express their gratitude and their commitments. We must get these people on our campus ministry lists, along with all the other persons who form our natural constituencies.

We tried several ways of informing our potential donors about our hopes and plans. We had a breakfast for about seventy-five persons featuring a talk by our bishop, who expressed his enthusiastic support for our project. A friend in the advertising business produced an attractive brochure, which included a concise summary of our objectives as well as supportive statements by the bishop and the president of the university. Later in the campaign, we began a regular newsletter to inform our various constituents about the people and the programs constituting our campus ministry. Information can also be circulated through the diocesan paper, bulletin announcements, letters to constituents, the secular media, and personal contact. It really helps to have someone coordinate this public relations effort, preferably an expert.

Involving people in the project starts with getting a core group committed to the idea of a Catholic professorship. Ideally the group should gradually bring more people on board. Students can be mobilized to call parents to solicit their support. A group of faculty and staff members can make personal contacts with their colleagues. Many people should be involved in identifying and contacting alumni scattered throughout the country. Through these contacts, some individuals will surface and show special interest and willingness to be more involved. It is important that they understand the project and that their talents are used.

In fact, asking for money proved to be difficult for many of our volunteers. Our expert advisors had various theories on how to approach this task. Individuals give to persons they like or respect, so make the matchups carefully. Take time to cultivate potential donors. Figure out ahead of time the amount you hope to get from contributors. Do not jump over dollars looking for pennies, which suggests concentrating on the large givers. Do not go public with the drive until you have secured the support of the major contributors. Be aware of other fund-raising drives in your area that involve the same constituency. It is important to penetrate the network of givers within the community who contribute to each other's causes. Arrange to have the campus ministry leaders talk to small groups of potential donors before soliciting their help.

When our campaign led by local volunteers was struggling, we debated hiring a fund-raising firm. We decided against this in part because the firms we consulted were very expensive and did not have a clear plan for reaching our scattered constituencies. Anyone undertaking a drive should think seriously about hiring experts at the very beginning.

We did hire a professional to seek funds from foundations for both our professorship and our building project, but the effort was totally unsuccessful. Other campus ministry centers have been more successful with foundations, and this possibility should be explored.

Finally, it is important to recognize the contributions of all the donors and to let them know precisely how they are assisting the ministry of the church on campus. In our case, we played up the first course offering in our professorship, which gave our students exposure to nine of the best known Catholic scholars from around the country. We wrote to all our donors, thanking them for making this possible and inviting them to attend these lectures themselves. A press conference featuring the president of the university, the bishop, and the Murray family gained media exposure for the professorship and helped many of our supporters feel part of an important project. The president of the university also hosted a large gathering of our major contributors at his home as a way of expressing appreciation to all involved.

In our own fund-raising efforts, we made many mistakes. Despite our fumbling, we did succeed in raising the $500,000 needed for the professorship. I believe that many other campus ministry centers could do as well or better. Financial doubts should not preclude local initiatives or halt a movement whose time has come.

OUR FIRST YEAR

We did not wait until we had $500,000 in hand to start our professorship in Catholic thought. Using the interest on the $240,000 already collected, we organized a course for our spring term in 1992 entitled "Current Trends in Catholic Thought," in which nine visiting scholars shared the Catholic professorship. Thus, we had Richard McCormick lecturing on morality; Richard McBrien on the church; Anne Carr on Christology; Michael Novak on social teaching; Avery Dulles on faith; Lisa Cahill on sexuality and gender; Arthur McGovern on liberation theology; Lawrence Cunningham on spirituality; and Donald Senior on scripture. The visiting professors lectured on Tuesday afternoons, and on Thursday, I led a discussion of their presentations with the undergraduate students in the course. The Tuesday lectures were attended by over three hundred members of the public on a noncredit basis for fifty dollars. Approximately one hundred undergraduates took the course for four credits, which could be used toward humanities requirements.

This course proved beneficial in inaugurating our professorship, since the well-known scholars gave the project great prominence and provided good publicity. Members of the community who have some knowledge of the theological world were excited by the opportunity to hear these distinguished professors, and the undergraduate students were exposed to a tradition with valuable resources for their lives.

The success of our initial course suggests that there may be other creative ways of beginning Catholic professorships even before substantial amounts of money are collected.

SUMMARY

1. The establishment of Catholic professorships and chairs is a constructive way to respond to religious illiteracy and to pass on the Catholic heritage.
2. The idea is to collect a substantial amount of money and give it to the university as an endowment so that the interest on the principal can be used to fund the professorship.
3. Gather a core group of people committed to the project and gradually expand the base of support.

4. At the very outset, gain the support of the bishop and important administrators at the university, including the president.

5. Include the ecumenical and interfaith dimension by informing other campus ministers of the project and encouraging them to do something similar.

6. Coordinate the Catholic professorship with other religious studies programs already existing in the university.

7. Draw up a contract that protects the interests of the Catholic community and respects the complexities of the church and state relationship.

8. Concentrate on large contributors to the endowment fund while cultivating a broad base of support.

9. Finally, keep in mind that the whole project is for the sake of our young people, who need to gain an adult understanding of their faith to be effective participants in the church and the world.

DIALOGUE WITH FRANCIS

During his papacy, Francis has made it clear in deed and word that the church has a role to play in the public arena. He has encouraged Christians to participate in the affairs of the world, confident that we have something to contribute while respecting the proper autonomy of politics and economics. According to press reports, the pope played a role in the reestablishment of diplomatic relations between Cuba and the United States. He has said himself that he hopes his encyclical, *Laudato Si'*, will influence world leaders to take constructive actions to control global warming. He brought together Palestinian and Israeli leaders to discuss paths to peace. The pope does not want a church with a ghetto mentality that confines itself to the sacristy. Carrying out its proper role, the church must go out to the world, confident that Christ has a message that can help humanize our culture and create a more just society. Campus ministers influenced by Francis look for creative ways to influence the moral climate on campus and bring Christian perspectives to discussions in the public arena.

Before being elected pope, Jorge Bergoglio addressed the cardinals, calling for a church that goes out of herself by proclaiming God's word and that refuses to live within and for herself. In that talk, according to one of the cardinals, he reversed the usual image of Jesus knocking at the door of our hearts wanting to enter and spoke instead of Jesus already within knocking so that we will let him come out and take his message to the world. Some claim that this talk resonated with the cardinals and played a role in Bergoglio's election.

In *The Joy of the Gospel*, Francis returned to this theme under the heading of "A Church Which Goes Forth" (n. 20–24). He notes the great biblical figures called by God to go forth: Abraham, who set out for a new land; Moses, who led the Israelites out of slavery; and Jeremiah, who preached to those designated by God. Jesus commanded his followers to go and make disciples. Applying this general command, Francis says the community of believers is "called to go forth from our own comfort zone to reach all the peripheries in need of the light of the Gospel" (n. 20). The church goes forth with "an endless desire to show mercy," willing to abase itself as it "embraces human life" (n. 24). On various occasions, Francis has spoken of his preferences for a church that is "bruised, hurting, and dirty," because of its involvement in the world, rather than a church "clinging to its own security." To remain in the safety of the sacristy is ultimately suffocating for a church called to bring the fresh air of the gospel to a world closed in on itself.

Campus ministers who leave the comfort of the ecclesial world and go forth into the academic world to help establish chairs of Catholic Studies encounter the realities of university politics. They are confronted by power issues, turf wars, and ideological differences. They may have to contend with strenuous arguments against the proposal: it violates the separation of church and state; it introduces into the curriculum the topic of faith, which should remain a private matter; it gives the Catholic tradition an unfair advantage in the public discussion of religion; and it gives voice to a religion that is fundamentally dehumanizing. Arguing the case for endowed chairs in religion can turn friends into enemies or opponents. Success is often determined by cultivating relationships with major decision-makers and getting involved in the messy dynamics of the power structure. Developing contracts brings the church into the complex world of the First Amendment. Raising money can strain relationships with other organizations courting the same donor base and the same large contributors. Once a chair in Catholic Studies is established, there is the sometimes contentious process of identifying the best person for the position and then the challenge of persuading that scholar to accept the offer. Campus ministers reluctant to enter the complex world of higher education can find strength in Pope Francis, who encourages church leaders to go forth confident that Christ always accompanies his disciples.

VI

EDUCATING
FOR
JUSTICE

12

CATHOLIC SOCIAL TEACHING

The following material is derived from the second part of the earlier document, "The Quest for Wisdom." After treating the dialogic relationship between the church and higher education, the document examines the church on campus as a wisdom community that helps the members grow spiritually, form healthy relationships, develop into effective leaders, and work for social justice. The section on social justice, presented here, is a response to the excessive individualism rampant in the culture, apathy on campus, and ignorance of Catholic social teaching within the church. It offers theological perspectives and practical strategies.

WISDOM AND SOCIAL JUSTICE

The ideal faith community becomes a servant of the larger society. The members understand that "action on behalf of justice is a significant criterion of the church's fidelity to its missions. It is not optional, nor is it the work of only a few in the church. It is something to which all Christians are called according to their vocations, talents, and situations in life."[1] They realize that this teaching is rooted in the dignity and social character of all human beings. They find inspiration in the social dimension of the scriptures and the example of Jesus the servant (Mark 10:45) who came "to bring good news to the poor…to proclaim release to the captives" (Luke 4:18). This is the solid basis for their commitment to work for justice and peace.

The church on campus well understands that "knowledge of economics and politics will not in itself bring about justice, unless it is activated by human and religious ideals. However, religious ideals without the necessary secular expertise will not provide the kind of leadership needed to influence our complex society."[2] It realizes that education for justice and peace "requires teaching and learning the tradition of Catholic social thought, the creation of an environment for learning that reflects a commitment to justice and openness on the part of all Catholics to change personal attitudes and behavior."[3] In its effort to promote social justice, the community of faith draws on the wisdom of the Judeo-Christian tradition, the coherent body of social teachings developed by the church during the last century, and the latest scientific findings.

In the wisdom community, education must lead to a constructive action. The Gospel mandate is to fight against injustice and to work for the transformation of society. Individuals and groups must be empowered to take charge of their own lives and to shape their own destinies.

Finally, the community of faith realizes that "any group which ventures to speak to others about justice should itself be just, and should be seen as such. [It] must therefore submit its own policies, programs, and manner of life to continuing review."[4] The servant community on campus recognizes its call to be an authentic sign of Christ, the suffering servant.

STRATEGIES

Implementing this ideal means resisting the rising tide of excessive individualism in our culture. Some campus ministers report favorable results through forming coalitions. Examples include combining with other religious groups in sponsoring periodic fasts for world hunger; working with a department on campus to sponsor seminars on peace; encouraging students to join groups that work for social change; helping to establish a social justice committee on campus; and cosponsoring lectures on social questions.

Resources on campus can be utilized to raise consciousness on social matters. For instance, it is possible to identify relevant courses and encourage students to take them; to get campus radio stations to present programs on justice and peace; to gather international students to share their perceptions; and to organize interdepartmental seminars.

There are also ways to sharpen social awareness within the faith community. Social concerns can be addressed through thematic liturgies, homilies, and seminars. A social justice committee can keep others informed about the status of specific issues. Relevant articles can be passed out at Mass. A committee can be established to promote a consistent pro-life ethic. Some campuses provide an ongoing witness by tithing their weekly collections for various worthy causes. Faculty members with a competency can be made available to speak to students. Many campus ministers now place great emphasis on informing students about the dangers of nuclear war and the importance of working for peace. A knowledge of Catholic social teaching can be gained by studying the growing body of papal and episcopal teachings on social issues.[5] This teaching provides a consistent perspective that exposes societal contradictions and an ongoing motivation that encourages work on behalf of peace and justice.

Many parishes and centers provide opportunities for students to be involved in service projects such as visiting nursing homes, volunteering at institutions for people with disabilities, serving in local soup kitchens, helping in disadvantaged areas of the country during the summer, and tutoring in inner-city schools.

Despite the often disappointing general response to social justice programs, the community of faith must continue to remind people that "education for justice is a significant element in the general call to Gospel holiness."[6] Campus ministers often find encouragement in the small but committed group of young people who have a highly developed social consciousness and involve themselves in action-oriented projects for peace and justice. The true wisdom community keeps striving to become a genuine servant community.

DIALOGUE WITH FRANCIS

On June 18, 2015, Pope Francis released his highly anticipated encyclical on the environment with the Italian title *Laudato Si'* taken from the beginning of *The Canticle of Creatures* by St. Francis of Assisi, "Praise be to you, My Lord." Much of the early secular reaction to the 138-page document centered on the pope's unambiguous statement on the controversial issue of global warming: "a number of scientific studies indicate that most global warming in recent decades is due to the great concentration of greenhouse gases (carbon dioxide, methane, nitrogen oxides, and others) released mainly as a result of human activity." *The New York Times*, for example, reported that Francis placed most of the blame for climate change on "fossil fuels and human activity," with industrialized countries "mostly responsible." The article noted that the pope blames the "destruction of the environment" on "apathy, the reckless pursuit of profits, excessive faith in technology, and political shortsightedness."[7]

Defenders of Francis point out that he based his position on the work of the Pontifical Academy of Sciences, composed of eighty respected scientists from thirty-six countries with forty-eight Nobel Prizes to their credit. The Academy held a series of conferences on global warming and issued a final report that concluded "human-induced climate change is a scientific reality." The pope does not claim that the church has the power to decide disputed scientific questions, but his dialogue with climate experts convinced him that there is "a very solid consensus" on "disturbing warming of the climatic system."

Although global warming has drawn the headlines, the enduring heart of the encyclical, subtitled *On Care for Our Common Home*, is an ecological spirituality drawn from the Bible, inspired by St. Francis of Assisi, and grounded in solid theology. This spirituality serves as a radical response to the contemporary ecological crisis. Following a pattern endorsed by Vatican II, Pope Francis begins by reading the signs of the times, which reveal a serious worldwide environmental crisis. In the first chapter of the encyclical, Francis offers a cursory review of the degradation of our planet, not "to amass information or satisfy curiosity," but "to turn what is happening to the world into our own personal suffering and thus to discover what each of us can do about it." Our "throwaway culture," which "quickly reduces things to rubbish," has not sufficiently developed "the capacity to absorb and reuse waste and by-products," causing our earth "to look more and more like a pile of filth." Our supplies of safe drinking water are diminishing. Each year thousands of plant and animal species are lost forever. Tropical forests are burned down or levelled for cultivation, destroying valuable ecosystems. Uncontrolled fishing in rivers, lakes, seas, and oceans is leading to "a drastic depletion" of certain species of marine life. Many of the world's coral reefs are "already barren or in a state of constant decline."

Dismayed by the weak responses of political institutions to the environmental crisis, Pope Francis wants to promote a dialogue among all people of goodwill based on "a new and universal solidarity" so that all of us can cooperate in "the care of creation, each according to his or her own culture, experience, involvements, and talents." The Pope is convinced that the church can make an important contribution to that dialogue and cooperative effort.

As one response to the environmental crisis, Francis presents a theology of creation drawn from the Bible and placed in a contemporary evolutionary framework. In "symbolic and narrative language," the creation accounts in the Book of Genesis teach us that God is the Creator of all that exists, that every creature possesses a fundamental goodness and that creatures give praise to God by their very existence. Creation is a gift from God, whose love is "the fundamental moving force in all created things." In poetic language, Pope Francis describes creation as a "caress of God," and "a precious book" that manifests "the inexhaustible riches of God."

The first creation account in the Book of Genesis teaches that "every man and woman is created out of love and made in God's image and likeness." We are blessed with "an infinite dignity." Francis comments: "How wonderful the certainty" that we are "not adrift in the midst of hopeless chaos," but are sustained by "the special love of the Creator for each human being."

For Francis, Genesis suggests that we humans have "three fundamental and closely intertwined relationships: with God, with our neighbor, and with the earth itself." As the story of Cain killing his brother Abel indicates, sin distorts these fundamental relationships. In that context, the Pope recognizes that Christians have distorted the biblical injunction that man has "dominion" over the earth, using it to justify "unbridled exploitation of nature," as critics of biblical religion have argued. Responding to the critics, Francis insists that we must "forcefully reject" the notion that human beings have "absolute domination over other creatures." We are not God; we do not own the earth; and we have no right to exploit and degrade God's creation.

At the same time, Francis emphasizes the imminence of God who sustains the created world and calls human beings to participate in the ongoing process of creation. God is intimately present to all creatures. The divine presence "continues the work of creation," ensuring "the subsistence and growth of each being." The Spirit of God has filled the universe with possibilities so that "something new" can always emerge from "the very heart of things." God created "a world in need of development," thereby "in some way" limiting the divine power. The Creator has chosen to share the work of creation with human beings. The Father of all has entrusted to us care for "a fragile world," challenging us "to devise intelligent ways" of using our own power to help the material world evolve in a positive direction so that "freedom, growth, salvation, and love can blossom." Endowed with intelligence and love, we are called not only to protect creation, but to "lead all creatures back to their Creator."

This outline of a theology of creation presented by Francis establishes a solid foundation for an ecological spirituality that appreciates the beauty of the material world and accepts responsibility for protecting the earth. In developing this spirituality, we find inspiration and guidance in Jesus Christ, who lived in harmony not only with God and fellow human beings but also with the created world. Jesus used familiar elements of the natural world (for example, birds and flowers, seeds and harvests) to teach us about the reign of God. He assured us that God is our Father and has special care for each and every creature. Far from being an ascetic who "despised the body, matter and the things of this world," Jesus worked with his hands and was "in constant touch with nature, lending it an attention full of fondness and wonder."[8]

Pope Francis reminds us that "the destiny of all creation is bound up with the mystery of Christ." As the Divine Word, "all things have been created through him and for him" (Col 1:16). Through the incarnation, the Word made flesh shared completely in our material evolving world, living "in full harmony with creation." As the risen Lord, "he holds the creatures of this world to himself, directing them toward fullness as their end." An ecological spirituality inspired by Christ appreciates the beauty of creation, learns from nature, treats the world with loving care, and cooperates in the task of leading creatures to their proper end.

The spirituality of *Laudato Si'* is thoroughly Franciscan. It begins with a line from *The Canticle of Creatures* composed by St. Francis of Assisi: "Praise be to you, my Lord, through our Sister, Mother Earth, who sustains and governs us, and who produces various fruit with colored flowers and herbs." Other references to the saint from Assisi are scattered through the encyclical. In one place, Pope Francis describes St. Francis in glowing terms: an "attractive and compelling figure;" "my guide and inspiration;" "the example par excellence" of an "integral ecology lived out joyfully and authentically;" "a mystic and a pilgrim who lived in simplicity and in wonderful harmony with God, with others, with nature and with himself." Saint Francis invites us "to see nature as a magnificent book in which God speaks to us and grants us a glimpse of his infinite beauty and goodness." The pope also raises up the figure of St. Bonaventure, a major architect of Franciscan spirituality, who invites us to be on alert for vestiges or footprints of the triune God in our own inner life and in the world of nature. We can also detect the influence of the great Franciscan theologian, John Duns Scotus, who taught that God loves each creature in its unique individuality. An ecological spirituality, steeped in the Franciscan tradition, resists the temptation "to turn reality into an object simply to be used and controlled," while approaching nature with a sense of "awe and wonder," ready to protect and care for God's gift of creation.

Reflecting advances in contemporary moral theology and spirituality, Pope Francis puts great emphasis on developing "ecological virtues," which incline us to simplify our lifestyle and to live in harmony with the created world. The pope speaks of "an attitude of the heart" that "approaches life with serene attentiveness," is "fully present" to other people, and "accepts each moment as a gift from God to be lived to the full." A balanced lifestyle combines work, which serves as "a path to growth, human development and personal fulfilment," and proper leisure that renews our spirits and "opens our eyes" to the true meaning of life. For Francis, the Eucharist, which is "an act of cosmic love" joining heaven and earth, inspires and nourishes an eco-spirituality, serving as "a source of light and motivation for our concerns for the environment, directing us to be stewards of all creation."

The ecological virtues incline people to make environmentally healthy decisions. Francis lists some examples: "avoiding the use of plastic and paper, reducing water consumption, separating refuse, cooking only what can reasonably be consumed, care for other living beings, using public transport or car-pooling, planting trees, turning off unnecessary lights."[9] This kind of simple activity, "done for the right reason," can be "an act of love" and can, he believes, "directly and significantly affect the world around us." Thus, Pope Francis assures ordinary people that we can make a difference and offers us hope that our political leaders can achieve the kind of institutional reforms and international agreements needed to save and protect our common home, our Sister, Mother Earth.

Laudato Si', with its theology of creation and Franciscan spirituality, is a great gift to campus ministry. It appeals to the ecological sensibilities found in a growing number of millennial collegians today. They have grown up with an incipient awareness of our environmental problems. Many of them are familiar with discussions of global warming and are in the habit of recycling. Their frame for thinking about ecology comes largely from the secular world, shaped by science, mass communications, and social media. Campus ministers have a wonderful opportunity to tap this interest and to introduce the spiritual framework proposed by Francis. The celebrity status of the pope makes that broader perspective more available and more attractive. Campus ministers can employ religious language that correlates with the broad spiritual outlook of many collegians: God is the one who calls us to cocreate the evolving world; Christ is the God-man who lived in harmony with nature; the Holy Spirit is the gift who draws us into a community of creatures. Our secular culture with its ecological concerns has generated a pre-evangelization that is fundamentally open to a Christian ecological spirituality. Furthermore, Francis has provided a way to generate interest in social justice by linking it with environmental justice. Hearing the cries of Mother Earth suffering from global warming prepares us to hear the cries of the poor and marginalized suffering from injustice and poverty. The brilliant analysis of Francis, which demonstrates the essential connection between environmental and social ecology, can be turned to advantage as campus ministry attempts to overcome apathy and get more collegians involved in social issues. All signs point to Pope Francis making a significant impact on the ministerial function of Educating for Justice, which is really a call to action.

13

COLLEGIANS FOR JUSTICE

In 1994, Oxfam America, a relief and development organization dedicated to helping poor people in the developing countries, began the Fast for a World Harvest, designed to raise awareness of the plight of the hungry poor and to fund long-term solutions to social injustice, poverty, and hunger. The program, which seeks to overcome patronizing attitudes toward the poor, took hold on college campuses around the country, often with creative adaptations. The following article, written in 1985, describes the excellent work of the Corpus Christi Newman Club, which sponsored a successful fast on the University of Toledo campus. It is a fine example of a concrete way to carry out the ministerial function of educating for justice.

PEER MINISTERS WORKING FOR JUSTICE

On many campuses, the Thursday before Thanksgiving is designated as a "Fast for World Harvest." Students give up a meal, donating the money saved to help feed poor people around the world. In addition, educational programs help raise consciousness on the extent of the problem as well as the possibilities of doing something about it.

For the past four years at the University of Toledo, members of our parish social justice committee have spearheaded the effort to involve the general student population in the Fast. The committee, composed of collegians committed to justice and peace, met regularly for months to plan all the details. They found joint sponsors among other student organizations. They negotiated with the food-services

191

company so that the maximum amount of money would be given to the hungry for each meal skipped. The Fast was advertised throughout the campus, urging students to make sacrifices for the less fortunate. Last year, about 450 students out of a resident population of 1,800 participated in it. The justice committee planned various educational and consciousness-raising activities on that day. A movie graphically portrayed the problem of hunger in Africa. Speakers with firsthand knowledge of the situation called for active involvement in responding to the plight of the poor. The leaders encouraged other students to join such organizations as Bread for the World and to write members of Congress on behalf of legislation benefiting the hungry. On the days preceding the Fast, students gathered for late evening prayer services to reflect on the meaning of the Gospel in a world so sharply divided into the affluent few and the poor majority. The Fast included a "hunger banquet," at which a few students ate sumptuously while most had a bowl of rice and a glass of water. Afterward, group discussions, well-prepared handouts, and a stimulating speaker helped to focus the meaning of the hunger banquet, giving at least a tiny inkling of the inequities that so many must endure every day of their lives.

The students who planned the Fast for World Harvest on our campus are a good example of peer ministers working for justice. Most of them are involved in projects throughout the year that promote justice, peace, and the respect for life.

Certainly, throughout the country there is a great deal of apathy among collegians about matters of social justice. At the same time, on most campuses there remains a small group of students committed to social causes. Many of the churches on campus have a social justice committee that attempts to keep alive the ideals of justice and peace. It is a hopeful sign that the recently reconstituted National Catholic Student Coalition has put such great emphasis on peace and justice issues. During my years in campus ministry, I have been impressed by individual students who not only were involved in social causes on campus but have also maintained their commitments to justice as adult participants in society. Less impressive, but still noteworthy, are the periodic waves of protest that sweep our campuses. Demonstrations against apartheid policies in South Africa, for example, continue to elicit substantial student responses, producing in the process a few leaders who remain serious about the cause.

Peer ministers committed to justice are a valuable resource

deserving of support and encouragement. They are not only few, but are subject to great disappointments as they encounter student apathy and the seemingly intractable character of the great social problems. The general commitment of the faith community to peace and justice is crucial to creating a supportive climate for social activists. To accomplish this in our university parish, we tithe the collection each week, donating the money to a charitable organization or cause. The recipient is announced ahead of time and is included in our prayers at Mass. We also make the works of justice and peace more visible by reporting the efforts of our social justice committee and announcing the various rallies and educational opportunities available in the area. Our peer ministers especially appreciate the prayers and personal words of encouragement offered by other parishioners.

Students involved in the works of justice learn greatly about the practical difficulties of opposing entrenched patterns of injustice. They are also enriched by their interaction with oppressed and suffering individuals. It is common for peer ministers to report that they received more than they gave in serving those in need. Nevertheless, these ministers need support. Experienced campus ministers can offer support by working with students on projects. Faculty members can provide information and perspective on controversial issues. Involved students need opportunities to express their frustration and to celebrate their successes. Group discussions at the end of a project allow peer ministers to reflect on the deep significance of their struggles against injustice. Common prayer encourages them to commend their efforts to God.

Contemporary liberation theology provides a context for understanding the works of justice. This theology, developed among oppressed people, encourages us to read the scriptures from the viewpoint of the poor and those on the margins of society. God appears as the architect of the exodus, freeing his people from slavery of the tyrant and giving them political, economic, and social freedom. The great prophets of Israel, such as Amos, emerge as champions of the poor by challenging the established powers.

In the twentieth century, the Catholic hierarchy has developed a coherent body of social teaching that applies general biblical norms to the concrete problems of the contemporary world. These social teachings include papal encyclicals such as Pope John XXIII's *Pacem in Terris* and pastoral letters of the American bishops such as *The Challenge of Peace: God's Promise and Our Response*. It is important for Catholic peer ministers to be aware of this body of social teaching. Effectiveness in the social apostolate is based on the ability to relate religious principles to concrete problems. Students who hope to do effective work for justice throughout their lives are well advised to begin this process during their collegiate years.

DIALOGUE WITH FRANCIS

Laudato Si' not only provides campus ministers with an environmental spirituality, it also offers an integral ecology that promotes the well-being of the entire human family. As Pope Francis has stated, the world is facing a single urgent crisis with two dimensions: the degradation of the environment by global warming, pollution, depletion of resources, and the extinction of species; and the exploitation of human beings trapped in poverty and denied the secure setting needed for full personal development and a healthy communal life. While many commentators recognize them as separate problems, Francis insists that they are essentially united and organically connected so that they influence one another. The poor suffer most from environmental disasters. The hungry are hurt most by soil erosion. Marginalized people are most likely to become refugees due to climate change. By the same token, when people are lifted out of poverty, they can be more attentive to caring for their surroundings. When marginalized people are integrated into a healthy communal life, they can contribute to the crucial task of caring for our common home.

Recognizing that "all creatures are connected," an integral ecology is attuned to the mysterious "network of relations" between human beings and their environment. An integral approach promotes "human ecology," dedicated to creating a healthy communal life for all people, and an "environmental ecology," committed to caring for the earth and protecting it. Since the world is facing a single unified crisis with two interconnected aspects, we need to find comprehensive solutions that take both concerns into account.

In reading the signs of the times, Pope Francis detects a "decline in the quality of human life," the unruly growth of cities with "visual pollution and noise," and congested neighborhoods lacking in "green space." Technological innovations, which have accomplished much good, have also contributed to increased violence, social aggression, and drug trafficking. The omnipresent digital world can impede people from "learning how to live wisely, to think deeply and to love generously." The electronic world, which facilitates communications, can also "shield us from direct contact with the pain, the fears and the joys of others and the complexity of their personal experiences."[1] The lack of physical encounters between the affluent powerful and the marginalized poor impoverishes both groups, leaving the poor invisible and the rich unmoved. In poor southern countries, "access to ownership of goods and resources for meeting vital needs is inhibited by a system of commercial relations and ownership which is structurally perverse." An integral ecology must be attentive to both the degradation of the earth and the cries of the poor.

Searching for the root causes of our united ecological problems, Francis assigns blame to what he calls "the technocratic paradigm," an undifferentiated one-dimensional way of viewing our relationship to the world that celebrates human control over material objects. This creates a confrontational relationship between the earth and human beings who accept "the lie" that there is an infinite supply of the world's goods that can be "squeezed dry beyond every limit." In this outlook, the method and aims of science and technology become the only way of attaining truth and managing the world. Technology tends to absorb everything into its "ironclad logic," which seeks power and lordship over all. This paradigm celebrates the free market and economic growth without concern for its potentially negative impact on human beings and the natural world. Reliance on technology to solve our problems blinds us to the larger picture and more creative solutions. It creates a "consumerist mentality" that privileges having over being, placing greater value on accumulating possessions than on personal growth.

The pope insists that to "generate resistance to the assault of the technocratic paradigm," we need a distinctive way of thinking about public policies, educational programs, and various lifestyles. We might call this combination a "spiritual paradigm" that challenges the technocratic paradigm, or as an ecological mind-set that challenges the consumerist mind-set.

A more spiritual approach to our ecological crisis can be grounded in a Christian anthropology. As Francis insists, we humans are characterized by fundamental relationships to God, other persons, and nature. We are not God and we did not create ourselves. We are totally dependent on the God who sustains us and is worthy of adoration. The Creator calls us to share in the ongoing task of creating our unfinished, evolving world.

All human beings are made in the image and likeness of God, which means we possess an inherent dignity, are worthy of respect, and have the right to be included. As children of the Father, we are brothers and sisters to one another. All humans are always subjects and should never be reduced to objects. We must treat every other person as a thou and not an it. As members of the human family, we are responsible for one another. Following the example and teachings of Jesus, we are to love our neighbor as ourselves, a command that extends to enemies as well as those pushed to the margins and trapped in a circle of poverty. We are all members of a universal family, "a sublime communion" joined by "unseen hands," which grounds our moral obligation to exclude no one from our compassion and care. This communion extends over time, creating an "intergenerational solidarity" that obliges us to care for the earth so that it is available in its beauty and richness for those who come after us.

Through our bodies, we are organically related to the material world. We are members of the community of creatures. We come from the earth and return to it. The fate of the human family is essentially connected to the fate of the earth. The beauty of the natural world reveals to us something of the beauty of the Creator. As Francis puts it: "Rather than a problem to be solved, the world is a joyful mystery to be contemplated with gladness and joy." As Christians, our sense of being intimately connected to the earth is supported and focused by our belief in the incarnation, that the Word became flesh in Jesus of Nazareth, who walked our earth and delighted in God's creation.

For Francis, "there is no ecology without an anthropology." Some theologians argue that his position would be strengthened by including the common universe story shared by all humans. We are the product of a 13.7-billion-year history. We are stardust become conscious of itself. We are the leading edge of the evolutionary process, now responsible for its future progress. Apart from the universe story, the relational anthropology of the pope provides a solid basis for an ecological spirituality that lives out the demands of loving our neighbor and protecting the earth.

In contrast to the technocratic paradigm, persons formed by Christian spirituality treat the earth not as material to be controlled and manipulated but as a gift from God worthy of respect and care. Realizing that material resources are finite, they try to limit their consumption and support sustainable development. Rejecting the common belief that accumulating possessions brings happiness, they try to simplify their lifestyle and make good with less. Persons with an ecological mind-set can rise above the rugged individualism celebrated by our culture and make decisions based on concern for the common good, which Catholic social teaching describes as the sum of conditions that allow humans to flourish. They reject unbridled forms of capitalism as well as dehumanizing forms of socialism in favor of economic systems and policies that serve the well-being of all the citizens, especially the most vulnerable and least fortunate. They are not content to remain in their own political and social enclaves, but attempt to promote dialogue with those who are "other" and to make personal contact with them.

According to Francis, developing a spirituality that challenges the entrenched technocratic paradigm requires an "ecological conversion," a radical change of mind and heart, a new way of thinking and acting that combines care for the earth and love of the poor and powerless. To sustain this effort, we need "ecological virtues," habits formed by healthy family life, wise educational practices, socially responsible institutions, and, for Christians, a church attuned to the crisis of both the earth and the poor. Christians who have appropriated a spiritual paradigm can realistically face our urgent ecological crisis without losing "the joy of our hope." As Pope Francis reminds us at the end of his wide-ranging, beautifully written, faith-inspired encyclical: The Lord of life "does not abandon us, for his love constantly impels us to find new ways forward." In a final Christian prayer for the earth, the pope concludes: "The poor and the earth are crying out. O Lord, save us with your power and light, help us to protect all life, to prepare for a better future, for the coming of Your Kingdom of justice, peace, love and beauty. Praise be to You!"

Laudato Si' has already made an impact on campus ministry in the United States and we can expect that impact to grow. The encyclical is widely recognized as an important contribution to the long-developing tradition of papal teaching on social issues, beginning with *Rerum Novarum* of Leo XIII in 1891. Many campus ministers have seized the moment generated by all the media attention on Francis, and found ways to make the teachings of *Laudato Si'* better known: making copies of the encyclical available; drawing on it for homily material; and sponsoring lectures, seminars, and discussions exploring its implications. We can imagine the Catholic Student Coalition, which operates in four regions around the country, promoting a national student movement to study and implement the encyclical.

The ongoing ecological crisis is going to keep the encyclical relevant in the foreseeable future. It is vital that the millennial generation not only recognize the problem but support efforts to solve it. Campus ministry, inspired by Francis, will help them meet this challenge.

EPILOGUE

Our dialogue between Pope Francis and campus ministry has revealed the remarkable endurance of the American bishops' pastoral letter *Empowered by the Spirit*. The bishops have published more significant pastorals, such as *The Challenge of Peace*, but few rival *Empowered by the Spirit* in active longevity. For over thirty years, it has had a direct influence on the way the American church has ministered to collegians, the future leaders of church and country. This remarkable reality was clear when the campus ministers of Pennsylvania invited me to give the keynote talk at their 2015 state convention honoring the thirtieth anniversary of the publication of the pastoral letter.

Eventually, the American bishops will publish a new pastoral letter on campus ministry. Times change; fresh cultural patterns emerge; new societal challenges appear; the self-understanding of the church develops; innovative pastoral practices gain momentum. This book demonstrates some possibilities of how Francis has already significantly enriched the church on campus and how we might take that process further.

In a relatively brief period, Pope Francis has become an international icon, now serving as a moral and spiritual guide not only for Catholics but for many others as well. His popularity is based on the common perception that he is an authentic human being and a credible witness to the inherent power of the Christian message. His symbolic gestures—for example, washing the feet of a Muslim girl—resonate with people because they seem to be genuine expressions of his inner spirit. His interactions with wounded and marginalized persons proclaim the truth of the gospel apart from any doctrinal statements or theological explanations. His symbolic actions are the message.

Francis does not provide us with a systematic theological framework for examining current questions. He is not a professional theologian, but he has excellent pastoral sensibilities rooted in solid theological principles. He is at his best when he relates fundamental gospel truths to concrete existential concerns. His consistently joyful and positive tone reinforces the power of his message.

In this book, the sections "Dialogue with Francis" draw on his thoughts and practices that are most relevant for campus ministry today. They are presented in their best light without any critical examination, concentrating on their practical applications. Admittedly, these thirteen sections do not comprise a comprehensive summary of the pope's teaching, nor do they make explicit the general themes of his pastoral practice. They do contain, however, several positive features: summaries of important parts of *Laudato Si'* and *The Joy of the Gospel*, which Francis wants better known; indications of his broad vision of a reformed church reaching out to those on the periphery; applications of his distinctive theological insights such as the cosmic nature of the liturgy; practical suggestions for more creative ministry; and the many signs of hope he detects in our world today.

It is important to recognize potential dangers of this generally uncritical appropriation of Pope Francis and his teachings. One such danger might be called an "ongoing papalism," inherited from the last two papacies, which relies so heavily on Francis that we forget that the whole people of God are responsible for the missionary thrust of the church. Campus ministers could be tempted to sit back cautiously waiting for further action by Francis, such as appointing more bishops in tune with his pastoral practice. They could, with overblown zeal, try to impose the teaching of Francis on their people: for example, his take on climate change that a sizable number of Catholics dispute. They could make too many references to Francis in homilies and lectures while failing to make clear the Christocentric character of papal teaching. In trying to maintain a proper balance, campus ministers should remember the concrete efforts of Francis himself to move away from papalism: appointing cardinals from around the world to assist in the governance of the church; making frequent references to national hierarchies in his teaching; allowing bishops to solve local problems better known to them than him; and consistently pointing away from himself to the Lord he serves.

Another danger is "papal politicization," which in this case means interpreting Francis in American political categories. During his visit to the United States, the secular media described the pope as leaning to the left and more in tune with liberals than conservatives. His support for environmental protection and care for the poor combined with his silence on domestic religious liberty controversies were interpreted as an endorsement of the liberal agenda. Although these political categories can illumine some aspects of the pope's approach and teaching, they can also obscure the theological base and spiritual thrust of his message. Furthermore, they can be used to draw Francis into our politically charged culture wars, which he clearly tried to avoid during his visit to the United States. He sees himself as a herald of the fundamental gospel message and as a teacher representing the Catholic tradition. At the same time, he welcomes a robust debate and honest disagreement within the church on the many ways of appropriating and applying the Christian tradition. The Gospel does indeed have political implications but people of goodwill can disagree on which public policies best reflect and implement evangelical values.

Aware of the dangers of papalism, campus ministers can enter a more fruitful dialogue with Francis. It is especially helpful to keep in mind his sense of the fundamental characteristics of the Gospel: its centrifugal thrust, which propels the church on campus out of the sacristy into engagement with the academic world; its humanizing power, which helps students move toward a healthy self-fulfillment; its joyful spirit, which makes the Christian life more attractive; its cosmic dimension, which links care for the earth with social justice; its communal sense of salvation, which grounds the ministerial function of community building; its emphasis on divine mercy, which enables campus ministers to deal with their limitations and failures; and its fundamental hope in God's promises, which encourages the community of faith to persevere in the great work of justice and peace.

Campus ministers cannot expect from Francis a comprehensive theological synthesis or specific pastoral strategies that fit the American campus scene. Not everything Francis has said and done is beyond criticism. For example, theologian Robert Barron, who was made auxiliary bishop of Los Angeles by Francis, has criticized the statement of the pope that God's essential attribute is mercy, claiming it is not mercy but love that was present in the Trinity from all eternity. Mercy is what love looks like, according to Barron, when it embraces sinners. Critics, both hostile and friendly, have pointed out flaws in the preparation and actual function of the two synods on the family. The attempt to elicit the views of the laity was not well planned or executed. The ten men on the drafting committee were not elected by the synod participants but were appointed by Francis. Most troubling, theologians were not involved in the synod process, nor were they consulted during the year between the two meetings. Of special import, feminists have criticized the pope's acceptance of a questionable theory of gender complementarity, which effectively limits the role of women in public life. They are also critical of him for not doing more to increase the role of women in the church. These examples suggest that campus ministers should not fall into the trap of papalism by uncritically accepting everything the pope says and does.

In the dialogue with Francis, campus ministers are in the best position to interpret and apply his example and teaching to the specific situations on their campuses. For example, inspired by the centrifugal thrust of Francis, the ministerial team at a thriving university parish could persuade the university to sponsor a Values and Ethics Week on campus focused on environmental concerns. Tutored by the pope, a lone campus minister at a small college could increase the low attendance at Sunday Mass by forming a liturgy committee that not only plans the Mass but actively recruits students to attend. Mindful that Francis is big on the practical applications of theology, the campus ministers at a Catholic university could organize a small discussion group where theology students could talk about what the material they learn in class means to them personally. Campus ministers will find the dialogue with Francis more beneficial if they think of it as a stimulus for their own creativity.

The people of God in the United States who admire Pope Francis and agree with his priorities for the church are looking for ways to propagate and implement his vision. Many of them are disappointed with the recent revision of the American bishops' document "Forming Consciences for Faithful Citizenship," published in preparation for the presidential election, because it does not reflect the pope's priorities, putting more emphasis on rejecting gay marriage than on caring for the environment and achieving justice for the poor. Those who support Francis must find various vehicles to carry forth his reforms. As we have presented, campus ministry, which touches large numbers of future leaders of church and society every year, is a prime candidate for transmitting the vision of Francis.

Epilogue

Since the publication of *Empowered by the Spirit* in 1985, the church on campus has helped propagate the spirit and teaching of the Second Vatican Council. Now campus ministers have an opportunity to engage Pope Francis in honest dialogue and to apply creatively his vision to the ongoing task of forming future leaders who appropriate the fundamental gospel teaching on love and are committed to caring for the earth and working for justice.

NOTES

FOREWORD

1. Martha Nussbaum, *Cultivating Humanity: A Classical Defense of Reform in Liberal Education* (Cambridge, MA: Harvard University Press, 1997).

2. NCCB, "Empowered by the Spirit: Campus Ministry Faces the Future" (November 15, 1985), no. 14, http://www.nccbuscc.org/education/highered/empowered.htm.

3. *Gaudium et spes*, no. 22.

1. BACKGROUND AND CONTEXT

1. For a later version of this material, see "The Making of a Pastoral Letter: 'The Quest for Wisdom' Revisited." *Journal of the Catholic Campus Ministry Association* (Spring 1987): 1–5.

2. "Involvement in Learning: Realizing the Potential of American Higher Education," *The Chronicle of Higher Education*, Oct. 24, 1984.

3. William Bennett, "To Reclaim a Legacy," *The Chronicle of Higher Education*, Nov. 28, 1984.

4. Ibid.

5. "Integrity in the College Curriculum: A Report to the Academic Community," The Chronicle of Higher Education, Feb. 13, 1985.

6. "The Quest for Wisdom," no. 4.

7. "The Quest for Wisdom," no. 26.

8. "The Quest for Wisdom," no. 28.

9. "The Quest for Wisdom," no. 13.

10. "The Quest for Wisdom," no. 34.

11. Ibid.

12. "The Quest for Wisdom," no. 44.

13. See http://www.vatican.va/archive/hist_councils/ii_vatican_council/documents/vat-ii_const_19641121_lumen-gentium_en.html.

14. Paul VI, *Presbyterorum ordinis* (December 1965), no.9.

15. Pope Francis with Antonio Spadaro, *My Door Is Always Open: A Conversation on Faith, Hope, and the Church in a Time of Change* (New York: Bloomsbury, 2014), 49.

16. Ibid.

17. Pope Francis, interview with Italian Jesuit journal, *La Civiltà Cattolica*, September 2013.

18. Ibid.

2. THE DRAFT DOCUMENT

1. "The Church of the University," *The Pope Speaks* 27, no. 3 (Fall 1982): 249–51.

2. Ibid., 251.

3. United States Catholic Conference, *Catholic Higher Education and the Pastoral Mission of the Church* (1981), 17, no. 32.

4. Ibid.

5. There are over 3,000 institutions of higher learning in the United States. The total student population is over twelve million, of which the estimated number of Catholics is over four million.

6. *Catholic Higher Education*, 10.

7. Paul VI, *On Evangelization in the Modern World* (December 1975), nos. 18–20.

8. Among the many consultations with administrators, faculty, students, selected experts, and others, we found especially helpful the close to three hundred responses received from presidents and elected faculty leaders representing institutions of higher education from all fifty states who informed us of their hopes and concerns.

9. In addition to the traditional institutions, an increasing amount of postsecondary education is offered by other organizations, such as corporations and research institutes. However, in this pastoral letter we are limiting our comments to the traditional institutions.

10. As a representative sample, see *Three Thousand Futures: The Next Twenty Years of Higher Education*, The Carnegie Council on Policy Studies in Higher Education (San Francisco: Jossey-Bass, 1980). [Readers of this first draft should note that it was completed before some major new studies on higher education appeared, including "Involvement in Learning: Realizing the Potential of American Education" and "To Reclaim a Legacy: A Report on Humanities in Education," which was written by William Bennett.]

11. For a schematic summary of generally agreed upon goals, see Howard Bowen, *Investment in Learning: The Individual and Social Value of American Higher Education* (San Francisco: Jossey-Bass, 1977), 55–59.

12. Admissions Testing Program, The College Entrance Examination Board. *National College-Bound Seniors, 1984*, 4. It should be noted that both the verbal and mathematics scores have risen slightly in the last couple of years. The fact that more students take the test now than twenty years ago should also be considered.

13. Bowen, 97.

14. Bowen, 119.

15. Ibid., 129.

16. For a helpful summary of this debate, see Derek Bok, *Beyond the Ivory Tower* (Cambridge, MA: Harvard University Press, 1982).

17. Bowen, 150–54.

18. *National College-Bound Seniors, 1984*, 7.

19. L. Ramist and S. Arbeiter, *Profiles, College-Bound Seniors, 1983* (New York: College Entrance Examination Board, 1984), vii.

20. *Three Thousand Futures*, 309–11.

21. "The Church of the University," 251.

22. *Pastoral Constitution on the Church in the Modern World*, in *The Documents of Vatican II*, ed. W. Abbott (New York: American Press, 1966), no. 12. [Hereafter all documents from Vatican II will be cited from the Abbott translation.]

23. John Paul II, "Address at Puebla," *Origins* 8, no. 34: 535.

24. *Pastoral Constitution*, no. 12.

25. Ibid., no. 10.

26. Ibid., no. 13.

27. Ibid., no. 14.

28. Ibid., no. 16.

29. Ibid., no. 17.

30. Ibid., no. 15.

31. Ibid.

32. Ibid.

33. *Declaration on Christian Education* in *The Documents of Vatican II*, no. 1.

34. Ibid.

35. John Paul II, "On the Family," December 15, 1981, no. 37.

36. *Declaration on Christian Education*, no. 5.

37. "The Church of the University," 250.

38. Ibid., 252

39. Ibid.

40. *Catholic Higher Education*, 2.

41. *Three Thousand Futures*, 119.

42. Ibid., 120, 124.

43. John Henry Cardinal Newman, *The Idea of a University* (Garden City, NY: Image Books, 1959), 158.

44. Ibid., 159.

45. "The Church of the University," 252.

46. *Catholic Higher Education*, 5.

47. Newman, 103.

48. *Catholic Higher Education*, 9.

49. *Declaration on Christian Education*, no. 1.

50. For the main ideas of this section, see David J. Hassel, *City of Wisdom* (Chicago: Loyola University Press, 1983).

3. A THEOLOGICAL COMMENTARY

1. For this history, see John Whitney Evans, *The Newman Movement* (Notre Dame: University of Notre Dame Press, 1980).

2. See Edward Schillebeeckx, *Jesus: An Experiment in Christology* (New York: Seabury Press, 1979).

3. See *The Shape of the Church to Come* (New York: Seabury Press, 1972).

4. For his most radical treatment of this question, see *Unity of the Churches: An Actual Possibility* (Philadelphia: Fortress Press, 1985).

5. For a good summary of his mature thoughts, see *Diversity and Communion* (Mystic, CT: Twenty-Third Publications, 1982).

6. This is not to idealize the collegiate experience, which obviously remains an ambivalent mixture of sin and grace. However, the campus experience does have a contribution to make to our overall understanding of Christianity just as any other expression of the faith does, such as the experience of rural Christians.

7. For the best summary of Rahner's theology, see his *Foundations of Christian Faith* (New York: Seabury Press, 1978).

8. For example, see Gregory Baum, *The Social Imperative* (New York: Paulist Press, 1979).

9. See Edward Schillebeeckx, *The Church with a Human Face* (New York: Crossroad, 1985).

10. See Karl Rahner, *The Shape of the Church to Come* (New York: Seabury Press, 1972), 112–18.

11. *Dogmatic Constitution on the Church*, no. 9.

12. Gerhard Lohfink, *Jesus and Community* (New York: Paulist Press, 1984); Avery Dulles, *Models of the Church* (Garden City, NY: Doubleday, 1974).

13. Avery Dulles, ibid.

14. Leonardo Boff, *Church: Charism and Power* (New York: Crossroad, 1985).

15. Avery Dulles, *A Church to Believe In* (New York: Crossroad Publishing Co., 1982).

16. For representative examples, see Bernard Haring, *Free and Faithful in Christ*, vol. 1 (New York: Seabury Press, 1978); and Charles Curran, *Themes in Fundamental Moral Theology* (Notre Dame: Notre Dame University Press, 1977).

17. For example, see Alasdair MacIntyre, *After Virtue* (Notre Dame: Notre Dame University Press, 1981); and Philip Keane, *Christian Ethics and Imagination* (New York: Paulist Press, 1984).

18. For the classic text, see Gustavo Gutierrez, *A Theology of Liberation* (Maryknoll, NY: Orbis Books, 1973).

19. For a difficult but helpful representative work, see Johann Baptist Metz, *Faith in History and Society* (New York: Seabury Press, 1980).

20. For a good example of Niebuhr's approach, see *Moral Man and Immoral Society* and *The Nature and Destiny of Man* (New York: Charles Scribner's Sons, 1941).

21. See Edward Schillebeeckx, *The Church with a Human Face* (New York: Crossroad, 1985).

22. See Karl Rahner, "Consecration in the Life of the Church" in *Theological Investigations*, vol. XIX (New York: Crossroad, 1983), 57–72.

4. IMPLEMENTING THE PASTORAL LETTER

1. See "Catholic Graduates: Striving for Religious Literacy," in *Jubilee 2000: A Gathering of the Church in Higher Education for the Third Millennium* (Cincinnati, OH: Catholic Campus Ministry Association, 1998/9), 1–8, written on the fifteenth anniversary of the pastoral letter with continued relevance today.

5. MILLENNIAL SPIRITUALITY

1. James J. Bacik, *Apologetics and the Eclipse of Mystery* (Notre Dame: University of Notre Dame Press, 1980).

2. Neil Howe and William Straus, *Millennials Go to College* (LifeCourse Associates, 2007).

3. Cf. James J. Bacik, *Spirituality in Action* (New York: Sheed & Ward, 1997).

4. James J. Bacik, *Spirituality in Transition* (New York: Sheed & Ward, 1996).

5. James J. Bacik, *Catholic Spirituality: Its History and Challenges* (Mahwah, NJ: Paulist Press, 2002).

6. James J. Bacik, *The Gracious Mystery* (Cincinnati, OH: St. Anthony Messenger Press, 1987).

7. Ernest L. Boyer, *Campus Life: In Search of Community*, special report; Carnegie Foundation for the Advancement of Teaching (San Francisco: Jossey-Bass Inc., 1990).

7. PEER MINISTRY

1. See "Peer Ministry," in *Community and Social Support for College Students*, ed. Norman S. Giddan (Charles C. Thomas, 1988), reprinted here with permission of the publisher.
2. Thomas O'Meara, *Theology of Ministry* (Mahwah, NJ: Paulist Press, 1999), 142.

8. AN EXPERIENCE OF COMMUNITY

1. *Empowered by the Spirit*, no. 37.
2. Pope Francis, "Apostolic Journey to Rio De Janeiro on the Occasion of the XXVIII World Youth Day, Address of Pope Francis," Saturday, July 28, 2013, https://w2.vatican.va/content/francesco/en/speeches/2013/july/documents/papa-francesco_20130727_gmg-episcopato-brasile.html#_ftn10.
3. Martin Luther King Jr., "Loving Your Enemies," sermon delivered at Dexter Avenue Baptist Church, November 17, 1957.

9. NEWMAN CLUBS REVISITED

1. See "Newman Clubs Revisited," *Gathering* (March–April 1986): 1.
2. Pope Francis, Ceremony Commemorating the 50th Anniversary of the Institution of the Synod of Bishops, Saturday, October 17, 2015, http://w2.vatican.va/content/francesco/en/speeches/2015/october/documents/papa-francesco_20151017_50-anniversario-sinodo.html.
3. See Second Vatican Council, Pastoral Constitution *Gaudium et spes* (December 7, 1965), 1.
4. Pope Francis, Ceremony Commemorating the 50th Anniversary of the Institution of the Synod of Bishops.
5. Ibid.
6. John Thavis, "Pope says synod is a 'listening' event; as guarantor of unity, pope has last word," *La Stampa*, October 17, 2015, http://www.lastampa.it/2015/10/17/vaticaninsider/eng/the-vatican/pope-says-synod-is-a-listening-event-as-guarantor-of-unity-pope-has-last-word-P6RpPup5wYMf7FZe2Vq27L/pagina.html.
7. Pope Francis, *Evangelii Gaudium*, no.32.
8. Pope Francis, Ceremony Commemorating the 50th Anniversary of the Institution of the Synod of Bishops.

10. STRIVING FOR RELIGIOUS LITERACY

1. See "Catholic Graduates: Striving for Religious Literacy," in *Jubilee 2000: A Gathering of the Church in Higher Education for the Third Millennium* (Cincinnatti, OH: Catholic Campus Ministry Association, 1998/9), 1–8.

2. Hans Küng, *Islam, Past Present & Future* (Oxford: Oneworld Publications, 2007), xxiii.

3. See James J. Bacik and Kevin E. Anderson, *A Light unto My Path: Crafting Effective Homilies* (Mahwah, NJ: Paulist Press, 2006).

11. ENDOWED PROFESSORSHIPS

1. See "A Proposal for Establishing Endowed Professorships and Chairs in Catholic Thought," *Journal of the Catholic Campus Ministry Association* (April 3, 1992): 17–24.

2. See Michael Galligan-Stierle, *The Gospel on Campus: A Handbook of Campus Ministry Resources and Programs* (Washington, DC: USCCB Publishing), 82–89.

12. CATHOLIC SOCIAL TEACHING

1. *Sharing the Light of Faith*, no. 160.

2. *Catholic Higher Education*, no. 39.

3. *To Do the Work of Justice*, in *Pastoral Letters of the United States Catholic Bishops*, ed. Hugh J. Nolan et al. (Washington, DC: United States Catholic Conference), 1984, no. 8.

4. *Sharing the Light of Faith*, no. 160.

5. We call attention to our own efforts as a national hierarchy to address current issues such as the nuclear threat in *The Challenge of Peace: God's Promise and Our Response*, and the economy.

6. *Catholic Higher Education*, no. 8.

7. Jim Yardley and Laurie Goodstein, "Pope Francis, in Sweeping Encyclical, Calls for Swift Action on Climate Change," *New York Times*, June 18, 2015, https://www.nytimes.com/2015/06/19/world/europe/pope-francis-in-sweeping-encyclical-calls-for-swift-action-on-climate-change.html.

8. Pope Francis, *Laudato Si'*, no. 97–98.

9. Ibid., no. 211.

13. COLLEGIANS FOR JUSTICE

1. Pope Francis, *Laudato Si'*, no. 47.